Because He Said So

TAKE JESUS AT HIS WORD

Jeffrey B. Thompson

WestBow
P R E S S
A DIVISION OF THOMAS NELSON

Scripture taken from the Holy Bible, New International Version®. Copyright © 1973, 1978, 1984 Biblica. Used by permission of Zondervan. All rights reserved.

WestBow Press books may be ordered through booksellers or by contacting:

WestBow Press
A Division of Thomas Nelson
1663 Liberty Drive
Bloomington, IN 47403
www.westbowpress.com
1-(866) 928-1240

ISBN: 978-1-4497-1485-7 (sc)
ISBN: 978-1-4497-1486-4 (e)

Library of Congress Control Number: 2011926059

Printed in the United States of America

WestBow Press rev. date: 03/30/2011

Contents

Preface

You can experience a phenomenal increase in miraculous, physical healing and delivery from torment – IN YOUR CHURCH. This increase is not dependent upon following any formula. The anticipated increase defies any formulas.

Increases in miraculous, physical healing and delivery from torment will substantially boost the faith of those in your church who diligently seek God on these issues. Witnessing a miracle changes lives. The certainty that no human accomplished the result leads to a certainty God is real and is lovingly interacting with His people.

There is no need for any experts or outside consultants for your church to experience this increase. You need not wait for a healing evangelist or a "gifted" speaker to visit your church. You may "pass go and collect your two hundred dollars" without the intervention of anyone outside your church.

My wife, Nancy, and I have prayed for many years for others to experience the healing power of God and to be delivered from torment. In the last three years, we have diligently and voraciously studied and practiced in order to participate in the physical healing and delivery from torment that is prophesied in Isaiah 53:4-6. I am very happy to report that we have seen an absolute explosion of the miraculous. I am also very happy to report that each of you can experience the same thing.

The last three years have taught us clearly two important things about healing and delivery from torment:

- it is not us; and
- there are no formulas.

All the healing and delivery from torment we have witnessed are the sole product of God's power, not ours. To be sure, He lets us participate and co-labor with Him. To be equally sure, all the results are accomplished through His power and His alone.

We have no certainty why we have witnessed this enormous increase in participation in the miraculous. We understand only that we have chosen to take Jesus at His word and that He is backing His word with all the power of heaven.

We have come to understand that there is a vast difference between *impossible* and *improbable*. It is abundantly clear that any physical healing or delivery from torment is *impossible* for us to accomplish on our own. God's delivery of His compassion to His people is not dependent upon any power or ability residing in us, either by gifting or natural ability. We are privileged to have co-labored with God but the truth is, He has the only laboring oar. We are simply in the boat. And what a boat ride it has been!

I have generally understood *impossible* to include a large measure of *improbable*. *Impossible* is an adjective used to describe a situation or action which is "not able to occur, exist, or be done." If something is not able to occur, it would seem to be *improbable*. If something is not able to exist, it would seem to be *improbable*. If something cannot be done, it would seem to be *improbable*.

However, *improbable* is an adjective used to describe a situation or action which is not likely to be true or to happen. What is *impossible* for me to do will be likewise *improbable* to occur unless someone with the power to accomplish the task does it in my stead. If God has already determined He will act in a miraculous intervention in history, then what seems to be *impossible* is no longer *improbable*.

If miraculous, physical healing and delivery from torment are rare or non-existent in your experience, you will likely conclude the rarity of the experience arises both from the *impossibility* of your bringing it to be and the *improbability* that God, who is able, will, in fact, bring it to pass. The easy part of miraculous physical healing and delivery from torment is the certainty that these things are *impossible* for me to accomplish. Since they are impossible for me, I don't need to try too hard. Since they are impossible for me, my reputation is not on the line. Everyone knows I can't so I need not be concerned with how the results reflect on me.

The more difficult part of this equation is being certain that God is more than willing to bring physical healing and delivery from torment.

However, that certainty increases my willingness to pray for these results. I need not be concerned whether I can *persuade* God to do what he is more than willing to do. I need only ask.

What result would you expect if you were certain that God had already decided to heal His people? What result would you expect if you were certain God had already decided to deliver His people from torment? What if we could pray for physical healing and delivery from torment with the same certainty of God's will to accomplish these things as to accomplish forgiveness of sin?

We don't ask God to forgive us from our sins hoping to find Him in a good mood. We don't hope that God will "give us a break on this one." Why not? The answer is that forgiveness of sin is inalterably the will of God and the reason He sent Jesus to earth in a man's body. It follows that if physical healing and delivery from torment is likewise inalterably the will of God and the reason He sent Jesus to earth, we can have the same assurance of God's healing touch and power to deliver from torment that we have for a new believer who recites the sinner's prayer. Study Isaiah 53:4-6 and see what conclusion you draw.

The concepts discussed in this book have taken on new meaning to us in the past three years. We can testify that we have a keener sense of belief in God's Word and who we are in the kingdom. We cannot discern any formula for delivery of God's compassion. What we can tell you is that the explosion in miracles, signs and wonders in our experience coincided with our changed and enlightened understanding of the matters addressed in this book. We cannot conclude that our keener insights caused any change in experience. We can conclude, however, that our keener insights did not prevent the change in our experience.

We strive to neither formulate nor accept any theology which is based upon what God apparently did not do. We know no answer as to why sometimes it appears that nothing happens when we pray for physical healing and delivery from torment. We are not interested in any theology which attempts to explain away the huge promises of God. We refuse to permit any apparently contradictory experience to make us question whether Jesus meant what He said.

Jesus said, "Anyone who has faith in me will do those things I have been doing. He will do even greater things than these, because I am going to the Father." (John 14:12) If this statement is not true, throw the book away. Jesus either was *the truth* (John 14:6) or He wasn't. The one who claims to be the truth simply cannot lie – nor even be mistaken. It is the ultimate oxymoron to believe that Jesus is God incarnate and alive today giving life to all who believe and to believe that anything He said is not true.

We give no credence to any experience which appears to contradict Jesus words. We simply refuse to believe that our limited understanding could ever equip us to conclude that what Jesus promised did not occur. If we don't comprehend it, the problem is not on His end. We have decided as an exercise of our wills not to believe only in a God who is small enough for us to understand.

So, what about the apparent contradictory experience? We choose to believe that it is *impossible* for us to pray for those things which are consistent with God's will and have nothing happen. The expressed will of God is not dependent upon our powers of observation and understanding. We may not comprehend what happened. We may not perceive what happened. We know we are unable to perceive when God's gifts are given in embryonic form and must be nurtured into fullness through time. We content ourselves to believe that when He said it, He meant it. Those things that have the backing of heaven will happen.

You need not agree with any of the assertions contained in this book in order to have your sins forgiven and to experience a closer walk with God. Disagreement about these matters will neither threaten your salvation nor devalue your importance in the kingdom. However, we believe if you come to accept the truth of the matters addressed in this book a vast difference in the results of your prayers will coincide with that acceptance – just as it did with us.

CHAPTER ONE
Vastly Different Results

Nancy, and I have prayed for others individually and together since the early 1980's. From the early 1980's until 2001, we saw occasional answers to prayers, mostly played out over an extended period of time. From our perspective during that time, God was capable of making a major change but usually did not make that change quickly. We saw major changes by delivery from torment for people who would pray with us through a "healing of memories." That process always resulted in significant relief, but we saw nothing miraculous about it.

In 2001 we began praying with five other couples in Ruidoso, New Mexico. The group was diverse and included several current and former pastors, a retired CEO of a major publicly held company, and a couple who had a lot of maturity in the Lord. At first, we began our meetings with a meal, then a study and then prayed together for mutual concerns. We avoided global prayers and focused on individual problems and situations known to the members of the group. When we finished our second study the meetings evolved. First to go was the meal. While we continued to enjoy the study, the prayer was too sweet to cut short. We simply did not want to "waste" our time together eating and visiting. We wanted to get to the praying.

We saw some amazing results. God was certainly listening. We all felt something powerful was happening. When it seemed time to take our experience outside our group, we started discussing sharing our experience with church groups in the area and encouraging others to participate in similar meetings. When the discussion got serious, the devil attacked full force. A series of injuries and job reassignments kept us from meeting regularly and the group lost its fire. Four of the five couples ultimately moved from Ruidoso in a relatively short span of time.

Even in the midst of these powerful prayer gatherings, even when God was filling needs all around the county, we did not observe any miracles, signs and wonders. There probably was some delivery from torment but it seemed to occur over an extended period. We interpreted our experiences as mighty acts of God but did not consider that we had seen a miracle, sign or wonder.

While in Ruidoso, we were also part of a prayer team which was asked to come to the front of the church during services for prayer. Members of the congregation were encouraged to come forward for individual prayer. We did see some mighty moves of God for those for whom we prayed. However, it did not appear that anything other than gradual improvement of conditions and emotions occurred. We did not observe miracles, signs and wonders. There were multiple words of knowledge and words of wisdom provided by the Holy Spirit, but little else.

Everything Changed

In February, 2008, a new question popped into my brain. I cannot remember what I was thinking about. I assume it was a question God posed rather than one that I posed. The question was really simple. Do you think we see fewer miracles, signs and wonders than we want to see simply because we don't ask often enough?

Can you see the anticipation of failure in the very wording of the question? The literal words pre-suppose that miracles, signs and wonders are a hit and miss reality. God may be in the right mood – or not! God may be convinced to act in the circumstances – or not! The question basically asks whether we can overcome the drought in miracles, signs and wonders by going to the well more often.

The form of the question arose from my view of the "sovereignty" of God. I believed that since God is sovereign He does *what* He wants, *when* He wants. I convinced myself that I could not overcome God's sovereignty. He was going to heal super-naturally only on those occasions when He chose to intervene in someone's history. My part was simply to ask in faith. God's part, in His sovereignty, was to respond *if He chose*.

With that mind-set, prayers sound a lot like trying to change God's mind to become more involved in a particular circumstance. Can I "guilt" Him into action by reminding Him of His Word? Can I create sympathy for the person I am praying for by reminding God how much He loves that person and how faithful the person has been or how giving the person has been? What are God's soft spots that I can hit with a fervent prayer that might convince Him to act?

Man alive, was I wrong. God has already made up His mind on the subject of divine healing, miracles, signs and wonders. Jesus has already paid for our physical healing and delivery from torment. Jesus never refused to heal anyone – ever – for any reason.

Take Jesus At His Word

Jesus performed so many miracles, the whole world would not have room for the books to record them all. (John 21:25) Those miracles contained in the Word are included for a reason. There is a lesson for us with each account of Jesus healing someone oppressed by the devil.

What is the lesson intended in the account of the royal official's child in John's Gospel? The words *"The man took Jesus at his word"* leap off the page. (See Chapter Six of this book.)

In 2008, Nancy and I starting taking Jesus at His word. If He said it, we believe it. Oh, yes, we had always believed that what Jesus said was true. We simply had not seen much of it manifested in our environment. Many of Jesus' statements contain promises that we had not seen manifested in our midst. We believed the truth of Jesus' statements were manifested in the lives of others. We just didn't know who those *others* were.

In 2008, we heard Bill Johnson, the senior pastor at Bethel Church in Redding, California say that "We live in a culture of highly developed unbelief." That statement basically slapped us in the face and said "Pay attention." Bill Johnson also said "Jesus is imprisoned in the bodies of unbelieving Christians." "The Holy Spirit is in you and He wants out." (Bill Johnson, *Healing: Our Neglected Birthright*)

Now, God really had our attention.

We realized over a period of a few months we could change our way of thinking and take Jesus at His word. We studied mightily to escape a culture of highly developed unbelief. The availability of miracles, signs and wonders simply captivated our entire focus. Once we started on that path, things got really exciting.

Discovering "New" Truths

Through Bill Johnson's teachings we heard biblical truths in a different light. We were Bereans to the core. We *"received the message with great eagerness and examined the Scriptures every day to see if what [Bill Johnson] said was true."* (Acts 17:11) We found that heart-felt belief in the truths stated clearly in the bible brought a different result than simple intellectual agreement that the promises in the Bible are true.

Bill Johnson's message, which seemed so fresh and new to us, is actually ancient. Most of what he says is not original to him – and it shouldn't be since he is preaching the Word which doesn't change. The spiritual realities Bill Johnson emphasizes have been known to the church since the middle 1800's, at a minimum.

Bill Johnson emphasizes that miracles, signs and wonders are part of "the normal Christian life." Every believer should expect to participate in miracles, signs and wonders because that is what God is up to in our midst.

I confess that I "misapprehended" the word "miracle." I understood a miracle as something that occurs which does not have a rational basis or explanation in the physical laws of this world other than a direct intervention of God. I put an overlay on that understanding. I believed the entire concept of "miracles" included "rarity." It did not occur to me that miracles could and do occur "all the time."

It is no longer unusual for us to see miracles when we pray for others. Quite the contrary, if a miracle is not perceived when we gather in Jesus' name, the experience is impotent. God is still every bit as powerful as He was when Jesus walked the earth. Jesus is no longer operating under self-imposed limitations. The Holy Spirit who empowered Jesus resides in all believers. How can we not expect that God will act powerfully in bringing to pass His will, the delivery of His compassion to His people?

We are all called to participate with God in accomplishing His purposes. (1 Corinthians 3:9) Bill Johnson is fond of saying "God is in a good mood. He is up to nothing but good." If He is up to nothing but good, we should expect that He will be blessing his people today. We are called to participate in that blessing.

Belief and Experience

We re-discovered many beliefs widely held by God's warriors of days gone by. Acceptance of these concepts is not necessary to salvation in the sense of changing your ultimate destination. Acceptance of these concepts goes a long way to understanding the concept of *sozo*, a complete restoration of spirit, soul and body, which is discussed in Chapters Two and Ten of this book.

A Roll Call

Several great bible scholars who experienced massive displays of miracles, signs and wonders were born in the 1840's and then others were sprinkled through the rest of that century:

- A. B. Simpson (1843-1919);
- Maria Woodworth Etter (1844-1924);
- John Alexander Dowie (1847-1907);
- Smith Wigglesworth (1859-1947);
- John G. Lake (1870-1935); and
- Aimee Semple McPherson (1890-1944).

Widespread Agreement Among God's Warriors

In the relatively unsophisticated time when these great warriors represented God, they exhibited an amazing agreement on spiritual matters. Many of these insights seem to have been largely lost to the church in the intervening eras.

Believing each and every one of these concepts does not *create* any ability to participate in miracles, signs and wonders. However, believing these concepts corresponds with the vastly different results we have experienced. Believing these concepts certainly does not *disqualify* anyone from participation in miracles, signs and wonders.

These warriors agreed and emphasized:

- "The willingness of God to heal is, upon reflection, absolutely inseparable from any right conception of God's nature." (John Alexander Dowie, *Healing Ever God's Will);*

- "Disease is the consequence of sin and the work of the Devil and would not have been in this world had there been no Devil." (John Alexander Dowie, *Healing Ever God's Will);*

- "Sickness is an abnormal condition of the body and cannot be a blessing from God." (Maria Woodworth Etter, *Signs and Wonders*, Chapter XIII) (See also John G. Lake, *God's Way of Healing);*

- "Divine healing is the act of God's grace, by the direct power of the Holy Spirit, by which the physical body is delivered from sickness and disease and restored to soundness and health." (Maria Woodworth Etter, *Signs and Wonders*, Chapter XIII);

- Divine Healing rests on Christ's Atonement. (John G. Lake, *God's Way of Healing);*

- God's way of healing is a person, not a thing. (John G. Lake, *God's Way of Healing);*

- The Lord Jesus Christ is still the healer. (John G. Lake, *God's Way of Healing);*

- "Redemption from sin, sickness, and death constitutes man's deliverance from bondage of Satan and his kingdom, and establishes the Kingdom of Heaven." (John G. Lake, *The Ministry of Healing and Miracles);*

- "The Church has been negligent in one thing. She has not prayed the power of God out of heaven." (John G. Lake, *The Science of Healing);*

- "For this purpose the Son of God was manifested, that he might destroy the works of the devil." (KJV 1 John 3:8);

- "God anointed Jesus of Nazareth with the Holy Ghost and with power: who went about doing good, and healing all that were oppressed of the devil; for God was with him." (KJV Acts 10:38);

- "As the Father has sent me, I am sending you." (KJV John 20:21);

- Jesus Christ the same yesterday, and today, and forever. (KJV Hebrews 13:8);

- And these signs shall follow them that believe; In my name shall they cast out devils; they shall speak with new tongues; They shall take up serpents; and if they drink any deadly thing, it shall not hurt them; they shall lay hands on the sick, and they shall recover. (KJV Mark 16:17-18).

If you find you cannot agree with these concepts, examine your experience with miracles, signs and wonders. Those who believed and followed these things experienced massive displays of God's power and love.

Once we changed our way of thinking to fully embrace these concepts, Nancy and I experienced an incredible history of God displaying His power and love through miracles, signs and wonders. What will happen if you change your way of thinking?

"And these signs will accompany those who believe." (Mark 16:17) What you believe seems to have a huge effect on whether signs will accompany you.

Miracles Became Common Place – But No Less Amazing

Within a week of our first hearing teachings by Bill Johnson he was scheduled to be at Sojourn Church in Carrollton, Texas. Nancy and I were breathless to attend. What we saw simply blew our minds. Well over 100 people were miraculously healed during the two meetings we attended.

One of those was Nancy. She received a significant healing to her hands which were quite impaired by osteoarthritis in the PIP joints. She had already enjoyed nine surgeries on her hands and wrist and was the proud owner of several carbon-steel artificial PIP joints. One of the people in the congregation prayed for her hands. Gradually, over about 36 hours, she received significant improvement in flexibility and relief of pain.

Naturally, Nancy was delighted to report her healing to the bible study group we attended. That group was never the same. Prayers for healing broke out that night with significant results. We never attended another bible study with that group where any actual study took place.

Within a few weeks, we were lying in bed on a Saturday night. As I prepared to sleep, Nancy began crying. I was comforted that it most likely was not something I had done prompting these tears. She sat up in bed and, through the tears, asked what I would say if she told me God had just told her He would be in our home the next night healing people.

I said, "I would say we should report this to our pastor and open our doors." The next day we went to church early to meet the pastor. After we reported the "happening" to him, he said he was preaching on healing that day and would ask us to give our testimonies, Nancy's healing of her hands and the healing of my back which also occurred at Sojourn Church.

Following our testimonies of healing in the past few days, we were asked to pray for people at the front of the church. People with hand, arm, back, knee, leg and feet problems lined up to ask us to pray. Nearly each of those people received a miraculous healing while we were praying. Now, this was fun! Such a great percentage of those for whom we prayed received a miracle that I was concerned there would be no one left needing a miraculous healing that evening at our house. I was wrong.

That Sunday night, twenty-five people showed up at our house seeking prayer for healing. A high percentage of them were touched miraculously that night. Nancy and I laid hands on many who were healed. Others were healed while we watched from across the room. After nearly four hours, we were exhausted and most people had left.

We started praying with a totally different confidence for healing. We prayed for people in restaurants, in doctor's offices (the doctor, not the patients), in my office and in our home. A high percentage of those for whom we prayed were miraculously healed. We saw legs grow out, people with serious ankle injuries put down their crutches, injured shoulders restored, people with "defective" total hip replacements lay down their canes and walk without pain, immobilized ankles become pliable, and people diagnosed with rheumatoid arthritis refuse to take the prescribed medication with no ill effect. We could scarcely have been more excited. And we were just getting started.

The percentage of persons healed has stayed quite high – around eighty percent or more. The conditions for which we have prayed have progressed to more "serious" problems – with the same rate of healings. We keep pursuing. We keep asking. We keep looking and listening for what the Father is doing and try to do that. We are careful to no longer ask God to bless what we are doing. Rather, we seek to do what He is already blessing.

Yes, You Can

I want to be abundantly clear on one point – apart from Jesus we can do nothing.

> *"Remain in me, and I will remain in you. No branch can bear fruit by itself; it must remain in the vine. Neither can you bear fruit unless you remain in me. 'I am the vine; you are the branches. If a man remains in me and I in him, he will bear much fruit; apart from me you can do nothing.'"* (John 15:4-5)

All miracles, signs and wonders come from God and God alone. In the realm of miracles, signs and wonders, Nancy and I do nothing. You can "do nothing" too.

All believers are qualified to participate in miracles, signs and wonders.

> *I tell you the truth, anyone who has faith in me will do what I have been doing. He will do even greater things than these, because I am going to the Father. And I will do whatever you ask in my name, so that the Son may bring glory to the Father. You may ask me for anything in my name, and I will do it.* (John 14:12-14)

Participation in miracles, signs and wonders is accomplished in large part by changing your way of thinking and taking Jesus at His word. Manifestations of God's power are available to all believers, not just experts.

You should expect to witness demonstrations of God's power. They are the rule rather than the exception. Will you take Jesus at His word? He said that *anyone* who has faith in Him will do even greater things than what He did? Do you fit within the definition of *anyone*?

CHAPTER TWO
Change Your Way of Thinking

After John was put in prison, Jesus went into Galilee, proclaiming the good news of God. "The time has come," He said. "The kingdom of God is near. Repent and believe the good news!" (Mark 1:14-15)

Jesus proclaimed the "good news of God." The current emphasis in the church restricts the "good news" to the promise that we are saved (from hell) by grace through faith in Jesus. The "good news" most often is presented as a limited message, "You can change your ultimate destination from hell to heaven." Basically, the teaching is that you should seek salvation as a form of fire insurance. Fire insurance is good – I am just not convinced that fire insurance is available as a stand-alone product.

What about life insurance? Jesus said He came to give us an abundant life. (John 10:10) The life available to us comes from the indwelling of the Holy Spirit. This indwelling brings far more than fire insurance!

The "good news of God" is reported right there in Mark's Gospel. *"The time has come."* Jesus was on the scene changing everything in spiritual realms. There was no delay, no need to wait. *"The time has come."*

"Time for what?" you ask. It was time for Jesus to make available a completely new reality, entrance into the kingdom of God. *"The kingdom of God is near."* Jesus was not announcing two concepts. Jesus said it was time for the kingdom of God, which was near, to begin to rule and reign in our hearts. The good news Jesus was urging us to believe is that the kingdom of God was replacing the Law and the Prophets. (Luke 16:16; Matthew 11:12-13)

Jesus then said, *"Repent and believe the good news!" Repent* is usually taught as a verb dealing primarily with both feeling sorry (perhaps even ashamed) and changing my behavior to clean up my flesh. *Repent* is broader than that.

Repent deals with Godly sorrow, not worldly sorrow. The concept of Godly sorrow is vastly different from the concept of worldly sorrow.

> *"Godly sorrow brings repentance that leads to salvation and leaves no regret, but worldly sorrow brings death."* (2 Corinthians 7:10)

Repenting does not bring Godly sorrow. Rather, Godly sorrow brings repentance. Worldly sorrow does not bring repentance. Rather, worldly sorrow brings death. The fruit of repentance is salvation, leaving no regret. There is no lingering sense of shame and sorrow for the past. Repentance, then, wears a smiley face.

Repent, in this passage comes from the Greek word *metanoia* which means to change your way of *thinking*, not acting. A change in your way of thinking may well, and probably should, change your actions. We have a "chicken and the egg" problem here. What comes first? Changing my actions has not changed my thinking. Changing my thinking has changed my actions.

The tie between repentance and actions springs from the assertion that repentance leads to salvation, which we most often associate simply with an eternal change of destination. *Salvation* in this passage is the Greek word *soteria*, which derives from *sozo*, which means a complete restoration of body, soul and spirit. Restoration of my spirit accomplishes an eternal change of destination from hell to heaven. If that were the end of it, it is worth it. However, there is so much more.

Restoration of the body and the soul is also included in *sozo*. The concept of salvation in the kingdom of God is so much larger than we have been taught. Salvation is so huge it is important to not leave home without it.

Stated differently, 2 Corinthians 7:10 says Godly sorrow brings a change in your way of thinking that leads to a complete restoration of spirit, soul and body and leaves no regret. Now that is some good news!

Let's look at Jesus' command again. *"Repent and believe the good news!"* First of all, note that this command is one sentence. He didn't say repent only. He didn't say believe the good news only. He tied both of those together. We are to repent *and* believe the good news. In this context it is clear that Jesus is commanding a change of attitude and attention. He is commanding us to change the latitude of our attitude. Jesus' command, paying careful heed to the Greek language (the original language of the New Testament), is:

Change your way of thinking and believe the good news.

When are we to change our way of thinking? Jesus said the time is now. When are we to believe the good news? Jesus said the time is now. What is the good news? The kingdom of God is near. Jesus was making entry into the kingdom available, but not mandatory. Entry into the kingdom should be accompanied by a change in thinking from the Law and the Prophets to another reality.

Nancy and I changed our way of thinking in 2008. I cannot adequately express how exciting it has been to be *transformed by the renewing of our minds.*" (Romans 12:2) Paul tells us that the result of the renewing of our minds is that we will *"be able to test and approve what God's will is – His good, pleasing and perfect will."* (Romans 12:2)

No longer do we believe that we pray for others to change God's mind. Rather, we believe that we have learned His good and perfect will in relation to healing and delivery from torment. Jesus healed all who were afflicted by the devil. (Acts 10:38) God's mind is already made up – no need for change. Knowledge of His good and perfect will certainly has been pleasing.

CHAPTER THREE

Clarity of Thought on Supernatural Healing

A clarity of thought on the subject of supernatural healing emerges from study of the writings of those who have experienced massive displays of miracles, signs and wonders. I was quite surprised to find that, although my interest was new and "cutting edge" the concepts which became most important to me have been known for more than one hundred years.

Many of those engaged in the healing ministries of today agree that:

- God's way of healing is a person, not a thing;
- The Lord Jesus Christ is still the healer;
- Divine healing rests on Christ's Atonement;
- Disease can never be God's will; and
- The gifts of healing are permanent.

It is illustrative to compare the experience of those who believe these ideas and those who do not. Those who experience miracles, signs and wonders on a regular, recurring basis believe this theology. Those who do not believe this theology, by and large, do not have this experience.

It is not necessary to agree with these theological statements in order to be saved. Your salvation is not the least threatened if you disagree with one or all of those statements. However, it is true that believing each of those statements is not a *disqualifier* for participation in miracles, signs and wonders.

All Sickness Is From the Devil

We are strong believers in a phrase that is popular these days. God is good – all the time. And all the time – God is good!

John Alexander Dowie relied on two cardinal doctrines.

- "Disease, like sin, is God's enemy, and the devil's work and can never be God's will." (Dowie, *Talks With Ministers on Divine Healing*, Congregational Club meeting held in the parlors of the Y.M.C.A. in San Francisco as reported by G.H. Hawkes);

- "*Jesus Christ is the same yesterday and today and forever.*" (Hebrews 13:8) Jesus promised to be with us always, even to the end of the world. He is still as able, willing, present to us and longing to heal His people as He was when He walked the earth. He has not changed His mind. Jesus is still the healer. (Lake, *God's Way of Healing*).

There is a clarity of purpose that emerges when we recognize that all sickness, disease and torment is the work of the devil. Understanding that God is unalterably opposed to all sickness, disease and torment, precludes double mindedness in prayers for the healing of the sick and those oppressed by the devil. We need not spend one moment trying to persuade God that He should oppose sickness, disease and oppression – He already does – and always will.

Since all sickness, disease and torment is from the devil, we need not worry about interfering with God's plan by praying for healing. We simply do not believe that God puts sickness on any of His people to teach them a lesson. We refuse to believe that God is tormenting His people so that they will modify their behavior.

It is not consistent to believe that God will put sickness or torment on His people when He sent Jesus to pay the price to deliver His people from the power of sin, including sickness and torment. Jesus never refused to heal anyone who sought healing. He never questioned whether the particular affliction may have been the will of His Father. Rather, he healed them all.

No Exclusivity

Albert B. Simpson, John Alexander Dowie, John G. Lake, Maria Woodworth Etter, Aimee Semple McPherson (and many others) experienced massive displays of miracles, signs and wonders in days long past. Bill Johnson, senior pastor at Bethel Church in Redding, California, has a vast ministry today which experiences massive displays of miracles, signs and wonders. The difference in Bill Johnson's teaching and the lives of the others I studied is that Bill Johnson teaches that all believers should expect to experience miraculous answers to prayer, not just a select few.

My study leads me to conclude that I had a flawed view of spiritual gifts. Somehow I had adopted an understanding that spiritual gifts created an ability in the person receiving the gift that enabled that person to perform tasks that were unavailable absent the gift. If, for example, a person had received a gift of healing I expected that there was a measure of power residing in that person individually to bring forth healing. I now understand that view to be a significant impediment to participation in supernatural ministry.

The greatest impediment is the exclusivity fostered by that view. If I believe that only certain, select individuals have received the gifts of healing, I will not feel led to pray for the sick and tormented. Rather, I will direct that sick or tormented person to someone who has the gift. If I can escape participation by directing the sick or tormented to others, I have no responsibility in the kingdom to deliver God's compassion to his people.

Jesus Is The Healer

A common thread in the writings of all the people who have experienced massive displays of miracles, signs and wonders is an understanding that Jesus performs the signs and wonders they experience. The work is not done by the power of someone who has received a gift. They did not seek or desire a set of ideas and truths, a theory, a gift, a blessing, a healing, a sanctification, a thing or an it. They sought a relationship with Jesus. They followed His direction. A.B. Simpson put it this way,

> "Here, Lord, am I. If you want me to be the channel of blessing to this one just breathe into me all that I need. It is simply Christ, Christ alone." (Simpson, *Himself*)

To Destroy the Works of the Devil

Another common thread among these individuals is that all believed that the Son of God was made manifest to destroy the works of the devil. (1 John 3:8) Jesus did not come to *fight* the works of the devil. He did not come to *hurt* or *weaken* the works of the devil. He did not come to *begin a war* on the works of the devil. He did not come to *bring to light* the works of the devil so we would know who our enemy is. He came to *destroy* the works of the devil. Jesus did not lie when He said, "It is finished." (John 19:30) It is not acceptable theology to believe that Jesus did not destroy the works of the devil – all of them.

Healing and Delivery from Torment
Are In The Atonement

Divine healing is in the atonement. Isaiah's prophecy concerning Jesus is clear that the atonement includes a payment for our healing and a delivery from torment. (Isaiah 53:4-5) An atonement that delivers us from the power of the devil necessarily deals with *all* the works of the devil. The atonement is not limited to a change of destination from hell to heaven. It also includes delivery from the power of sickness, disease and torment.

Since the time of Martin Luther, the Church has been good at teaching that forgiveness of sin is available to all who believe, that saving grace comes through faith, not works. Physical or emotional healing – not so much. We believe that we are "saved" by grace by belief in Jesus. This salvation is a gift given through His sacrificial blood. We don't doubt that "God our Savior . . . wants all men to be saved and to come to a knowledge of the truth." (1 Timothy 2:3-4) Upon a declaration of faith, we fully expect to see a changed life, never doubting that the "sinner's prayer" will deliver saving grace.

Just like the change of destination from hell to heaven, supernatural healing and delivery from torment is a gift of God. We are slow to accept that the crushing of His body was a payment for our healing. Why? Why do we question that Jesus carried our diseases? (Matthew 8:17; Isaiah 53:4-5) We should legitimately expect to see a manifestation of divine physical healing which was already paid for by the beating delivered to Jesus.

Healing Cannot be Earned

Since supernatural healing and delivery from torment is a gift, it cannot be earned. Great freedom comes from the proper recognition of this healing and delivery as a gift. The person who is praying does not need to work to earn the gift. The person for whom prayer is offered does not work to receive the gift. If either person is working (by exhibiting the proper attitude, having a positive confession, aligning his mind with the word of God, etc.), they labor in vain. Gifts are given, not earned.

CHAPTER FOUR

Jesus Operated Within Self-Imposed Limitations

Jesus is now and has always been God. (John 1:1) Prior to changing my thinking in 2008, I believed that Jesus was able to do miracles, signs and wonders because He is God. A proper understanding of the source of extent of the power available to Jesus created a monumental change in my understanding of my role in the kingdom.

While Jesus walked the earth as a man, He set aside most of His prerogatives. He imposed these limitations on Himself. A proper understanding of those limitations helped propel us into a life including miracles, signs and wonders.

God is omnipresent. He is everywhere. Jesus, while walking this earth, was not omnipresent. He was not physically present in Samaria at the same time He was physically present in Jerusalem. This is but one example of Jesus intentionally setting aside some of His prerogatives.

Another example is that Jesus was not omniscient or all knowing. Someone who is all knowing cannot be surprised. Jesus was not only surprised, He was astonished. (Matthew 8:10) Someone who is omniscient already knows all things and cannot learn new things. However, Jesus learned about the condition of the invalid beside the pool of Bethesda. (John 5:6)

Jesus' actions were not principally designed to illustrate the power of God. God's power was recorded and well recognized throughout the scriptures prior to Jesus' appearance on earth. Jesus' actions were principally designed to illustrate the power made available to a man who is standing in right relation to God.

What do you suppose Jesus prayed about? What guidance and direction did He seek from the Father? Jesus had to rely on the Father to position Him where God was going to act and direct Him what to do. I believe that a lot of Jesus' prayer time was dedicated to discovering where God was directing Him to go next and who the focus of God's attention in that place would be.

A proper understanding of the source of Jesus' power for miracles, signs and wonders is critical to a proper understanding of what is available to all believers. Every miracle, sign and wonder performed by Jesus followed His baptism by John. When He came out of the water, scripture records the Spirit of God descended upon him like a dove and remained. (John 1:33) Peter explained the source of Jesus' power to Cornelius:

> *You know what has happened throughout Judea, beginning in Galilee after the baptism that John preached – how God anointed Jesus of Nazareth with the Holy Spirit and power, and how he went around doing good and healing all who were under the power of the devil, because God was with him.* (Acts 10:37-38)

Today, God the Son has complete power to heal the sick, raise the dead and deliver from torment. Jesus the man put aside these powers while he walked the earth. For Him, this was a significant *limitation*.

What was a limitation to Jesus is in no sense a limitation to us. Jesus' self-imposed limitation opens the door to understanding the power made available to us. If Jesus had not voluntarily limited His power and ability while on the earth as a man, we would not have discovered that the source of His power to heal, deliver and raise the dead came from the Holy Spirit.

Jesus relied upon the Holy Spirit for all the power He needed to accomplish what the Father desired. We have access to the very same power.

"Wait," you say. We are not in the same situation as Jesus. Surely He was able to heal everyone who came to Him because He was God. Since we are not God, we cannot expect to be able to heal anyone. That is solely God's province. The proper response to this argument is "Yes" and "No."

The "Yes": It has always been and always will be the province of God to provide the power to heal and deliver from torment.

The "No": Jesus the man had no power to heal. He could not raise the dead. He could not deliver from torment. He could not cast out demons. With His self-imposed limitations He stood before the Father as we do.

Jesus was the exact representation of the Father. (Hebrews 1:3) All the fullness of God Himself lived in Jesus. (Colossians 2:9) Yet, Jesus was made like us in every way. (Hebrews 2:17)

Why do I say that Jesus had no power to heal, could not raise the dead and deliver from torment. How, then, can I say that Jesus could not cast out demons. I say that because *Jesus said so.*

After the healing of the invalid by the pool of Bethesda, Jesus was questioned about healing on the Sabbath. (Don't the religious leaders of the day amaze you? Forget the fact that the invalid was healed. Let's be religious and question the day of the week rather than be astounded at the power of God.) Jesus gave them this answer:

> *"I tell you the truth, the Son can do nothing by Himself; he can do only what he sees his Father doing, because whatever the Father does the Son also does." (John 5:19)*

This statement deals directly with power and authority, not choice or volition. Jesus didn't say He chose not to do anything unless He saw the Father doing it. He said He *could not* do anything by Himself. If I take Jesus at His word, Jesus had no power to do anything by Himself. While He walked the earth, Jesus was completely dependent upon the power of the Holy Spirit, just like we are.

The healing of the invalid near the pool at Bethesda took place long after John baptized Jesus. John's baptism of Jesus is widely accepted as being accompanied by Jesus' baptism with the Holy Spirit. All of His public ministry post-dated this baptism.

Even after the Spirit came down on Jesus and remained, Jesus admitted that by Himself, He could do nothing. In order to heal, in order to deliver from torment, in order to cast out demons, Jesus was dependent on the power of the Holy Spirit. The power to do those acts was not personal to Jesus.

If the Holy Spirit was not present to act, Jesus got nothing done. The Holy Spirit was the source of the power to do those things the Father was doing. When Jesus testified that He could only do what He saw the Father doing He was admitting that unless the Father had sent the Holy Spirit to perform miracles, signs and wonders, there would be no miracle signs and wonders. It is God who performed the miracles, signs and wonders through the power of the Holy Spirit, not Jesus the man.

On the day of Pentecost, Peter said: *"Jesus of Nazareth was a man accredited by God to you by miracles, wonders and signs, which God did among you through him, as you yourselves know."* (Acts 2:22) Peter makes it clear that Jesus did not perform the miracles, wonders and signs. Rather, God performed the miracles, wonders and signs. He performed those miracles, signs and wonders by acting *through* Jesus. God was the actor, not Jesus. Jesus was the perfect vessel. Jesus was a perfect host for the *presence* of God. The Spirit *remained* on Him.

Luke, the author of both the Gospel of Luke and the Book of the Acts of the Apostles, was a physician. With his medical background, Luke is likely a trustworthy reporter of the nature of the healings he described. Luke recounts the healing of an invalid lowered through a roof on his bed to be placed in front of Jesus.

> *One day as he was teaching, Pharisees and teachers of the law, who had come from every village of Galilee and from Judea and Jerusalem, were sitting there. And the power of the Lord was present for him to heal the sick.* (Luke 5:17)

Luke knew full well that by Himself Jesus could do nothing. How did he know? Jesus told him! Luke also knew that when Jesus saw what the Father was doing, all things were possible. Thus, Luke records that *the power of the Lord was present for him to heal the sick.* Absent this power, nothing would have happened. How do I know that? Jesus said so.

Not only was Jesus able to do only what He saw the Father doing, He was very careful about his tongue. Jesus only said what He heard the Father saying. Jesus said, *"I do nothing on my own but speak just what the Father has taught me."* (John 5:28) Jesus did not claim to speak of His own authority. He claimed that the Father commanded Him not only what to say but also how to say it. (John 12:49)

Jesus was not guarding His tongue to avoid sinning by His words. He guarded His tongue because He recognized that His words had extraordinary power. Jesus said, *"The words I have spoken to you are spirit and they are life."* (John 6:63) Peter confessed that Jesus had *"the words of eternal life."* (John 6:67). If Jesus spoke it, it came to pass.

The Power of Prophecy

God's word, once spoken, has power to accomplish God's purposes. God spoke the world into existence. God's word has incredible power and does not return to Him void.

> *"My word that goes out from my mouth . . . will not return to me empty, but will accomplish what I desire and achieve the purpose for which I sent it.* (Isaiah 55:11)

What is prophecy? It is the word of God. If God didn't say it, it isn't prophecy. It may be an accurate prediction of the future but it is not prophecy unless God says it.

A prophet is only a spokesman, not an interpreter. Spokesmen, by definition, speak for others, not themselves. Spokesmen give utterance to words, ideas and concepts that have no reality unless authorized by the person sending the spokesman. Spokesmen have no power to bring their words to pass unless the one for whom they speak has that power.

In this context, let's look at a powerful verse from The Revelation of Jesus Christ.

> *"For the testimony of Jesus is the spirit of prophecy."* (Revelation 19:10)

The phrase *"the testimony of Jesus is the spirit of prophecy"* is one of those powerful truths from the Bible that I recognized as extremely important when I first heard it but was unable to comprehend. I knew something enormous was contained in that phrase but couldn't comprehend what it was. Merely uttering that phrase in our study group ushered in a nearly tangible awareness of the presence of God. The mystery continues to unfold as we continue to ask God for miracles, signs and wonders.

Prophecy, the word of God, changes the reality of the circumstances in which it is uttered. The word of God has the power and authority of heaven behind it. Prophecy brings the presence of God and all His power with it. It is impossible to separate the *presence* of God from the *power* of God. When Jesus knew the Spirit of the Lord was *present*, He knew the *power* of the Lord was available for Him to heal the sick.

What is the *testimony of Jesus*? I do not claim to have anything near a complete understanding of the reach of the *testimony of Jesus*. I am certain, however, that, at a minimum, the testimony of Jesus includes what Jesus said (His words), what Jesus did in biblical times (testimony of what Jesus did) and what Jesus is doing today.

In our experience, more miraculous healings occur while we are praying for others if the prayer is preceded by recitation of the testimony of Jesus. I have no explanation why there is power in giving the testimony of Jesus. I am simply reporting that the testimony of Jesus ushers in an *awareness* of the *presence* of God. The spirit of prophecy is released by recitation of the testimony of Jesus. Since Jesus is the same, yesterday, today and forever (Hebrews 13:8), if Jesus did it in biblical times, last week or an hour ago, we can be certain that what the Father was doing in the past is consistent with His will and nature and He will continue doing it today.

We have noticed that we have significantly better success rates with certain types of conditions. If we have recently seen miraculous healing of shoulders, we have great confidence that the next shoulders we encounter will likewise be healed. Can it be that the testimony of what Jesus has done in the prior miraculous healings creates an atmosphere by that spirit of prophecy that this particular type of miraculous healing is more likely to be repeated? From our experience, the answer seems clearly to be "Yes."

Before leaving the subject of testimony, let's examine another statement from the Book of Revelation.

> *"Now have come the salvation and the power and the kingdom of our God, and the authority of his Christ. For the accuser of our brothers, who accuses them before our God day and night, has been hurled down. They overcame him by the blood of the Lamb and by the word of their testimony; they did not love their lives so much as to shrink from death."*
> (Revelation 12:10-11)

This passage makes it clear that salvation, the power and the kingdom of God have come. We know that *salvation* (*soteria - sozo*) includes a complete restoration of body, soul and spirit. John tells us this full salvation has already come. There is available to all who believe in Jesus complete restoration of body, soul and spirit. This full salvation is accompanied by the power of God, acting in His kingdom and through Jesus' authority.

What was it that overcame the accuser of the brethren? The accuser was overcome by blood of the Lamb and the word of their testimonies.

The sacrificed blood of the Lamb paid the price required by the Law, *in full*. The word of the testimonies of our brothers relates to what Jesus has done and is doing in the lives of believers. The collective "word of their testimonies" is the testimony of Jesus, the spirit of prophecy. The collective word of our testimonies is a powerful force because it has the power and authority of heaven behind it.

CHAPTER FIVE

God Is In The Healing Business

In the realm of divine health and miracles of healing, it is important to remember that prayers for healing are not prayers to change God's mind. He has already made up His mind on the subject. God is now, and always has been, in the healing business. It is part of His nature. It is one of His attributes. He is *Jehovah Rapha'*. He is *"the LORD, who heals you."* (Exodus 15:26)

King David recognized this essential truth about God when he wrote:

> *Praise the LORD, O my soul; all my inmost being, praise his holy name. Praise the LORD, O my soul, and forget not all his benefits – who forgives all your sins and heals all your diseases, who redeems your life from the pit and crowns you with love and compassion, who satisfies your desires with good things so that your youth is renewed like the eagle's.* (Psalms 103:1-5)

God does not change. If He was forgiving sins and healing diseases in David's time, He is still forgiving sins and healing diseases now.

Sacrificial System for Forgiveness of Sins

In the sacrificial system of David's time, forgiveness of sins was obtained by a confession of sins and the offering of the prescribed sacrifice as payment of a penalty for the sin. Once the confession was made and the payment was made, the sins were forgiven.

Today, the order has been reversed. Jesus was the perfect sacrificial lamb who was killed on the cross as a payment of the price for the forgiveness of all sin. This payment was made once for all. (Romans 6:10; Hebrews 7:27; Hebrews 9:25-28) He will not repeat this action. (Hebrews 9:25) The Apostle Paul makes it clear that Jesus *cannot* die again since death has lost its mastery over Him. (Romans 6:9) All sin committed by anyone alive today comes well after the time of the payment. The penalty has already been paid, in full, long before the idea of sin was born in any living person today.

Isaiah prophesied exactly this result. He prophesied that God would place the sin of all mankind on his suffering servant, Jesus, who would settle the issue. "*The LORD has laid on him the iniquity of us all.*" (Isaiah 53:6) Isaiah also knew that we would get it wrong. He prophesied that God's people would consider Jesus as having been stricken by God Himself, not by us. "*Yet, we considered Him stricken by God, smitten by Him and afflicted.*" (Isaiah 53:4)

Isaiah makes it clear that Jesus was pierced for our transgressions – not His. The cause lies with us, not Him. He was crushed for our iniquities. There was no fault on His side of the equation. It was our iniquities which brought these consequences upon Jesus. It is clear that the price paid by Jesus was an advance deposit for the forgiveness of our sins today. Before the sins of today were ever conceived, the door to forgiveness was flung wide open and the entire penalty was paid.

Payment for Healing and Deliverance from Torment

Isaiah is just as clear that *surely* Jesus took up our infirmities and carried our diseases. (Isaiah 53:4) (Matthew 8:17) Just as He made a payment in full for the forgiveness of sin, He also made a payment in full for healing and delivery from torment. Isaiah prophesied "*the punishment that brought us peace was upon Him.*" (Isaiah 53:5) Jesus' physical beating he endured before being nailed to the cross secured *peace* for us today. Just as Jesus will not come again for another crucifixion for the forgiveness of sin, He will not be punished again for our *peace*. The price for our delivery from torment included in that concept of *peace* has already been paid in full by the punishment He endured.

The second purchase Jesus made by His beating was our physical healing. "*By His wounds (stripes) we are healed.*" (Isaiah 53:5) The word translated *healed* in this passage is *rapha'*, which refers to a physical healing.

On His way to the cross, Jesus paid the price in full for my physical healing today.

The payments Jesus made for (1) forgiveness of sins, (2) delivery from torment, and (3) physical healing were ENOUGH. Jesus thought of everything and paid for it all.

There is no need to change God's mind about any of those three issues. Since the payment was made in full and encompassed everything, even those things in the future, Jesus settled for all time the issues of sin, torment and healing. *"Jesus Christ is the same yesterday and today and forever.* (Hebrews 13:8) He was fully committed against sin, torment and disease then. He is fully committed today. He will be fully committed forever.

God had a special anointing for Jesus. Jesus confirmed that anointing when He read from the scroll of Isaiah.

> *"The Spirit of the Lord is on me, because he has anointed me to preach good news to the poor. He has sent me to proclaim freedom for the prisoners and recovery of sight for the blind, to release the oppressed, to proclaim the year of the Lord's favor." Then he rolled up the scroll, gave it back to the attendant and sat down. The eyes of everyone in the synagogue were fastened on him, and he began by saying to them, "Today this scripture is fulfilled in your hearing."* (Luke 4:18-21)

Jesus was sent to proclaim freedom, recovery of health (sight for the blind), and release from oppression. Peter explained it this way:

> *"God anointed Jesus of Nazareth with the Holy Ghost and with power: who went about doing good, and healing all that were oppressed of the devil; for God was with him."* (Acts 10:38 KJV))

Jesus healed *all* who were oppressed by the devil. He *released* the oppressed by *healing* them of their diseases and giving them the peace that passes understanding. The word translated *healing* in this passage is the now familiar *rapha'*. Jesus was the healer then, is the healer now, and will be the healer forever. For God to change His mind on healing, Jesus has to change. God has given his Word that Jesus is not about to change.

CHAPTER SIX

Why Jesus Came to Earth

Before 2008 I had a general, rather fuzzy, idea of why Jesus came to earth. I was aware that He had come as an act of God's grace to be the sacrificial lamb of God. I knew that through His death forgiveness of my sins became available. I also knew that He came to give me life abundantly. I didn't have a very good understanding of abundant life.

As part of our change of thinking, we really studied what John meant when he wrote, *"For this purpose the Son of God was manifested, that he might destroy the works of the devil."* (1 John 3:8 KJV) I remember wondering whether this statement was even possible. How had I missed this important concept in my bible reading until then?

Purpose of Sending Jesus

God had at least five purposes for sending Jesus to earth:

- to destroy the works of the devil (1 John 3:8);
- to save His people from their sins (Matthew 1:20-21);
- to seek and save what was lost (Luke 19:1-10);
- to bring life to the full (John 10:10); and
- to preach the good news (Luke 4:43).

Jesus Came to Destroy the Works of the Devil

The Apostle John puts it this way: *"For this purpose the Son of God was manifested, that he might destroy the works of the devil."* (1 John 3:8) The works of the devil include sin, sickness, torment and death. The really good news is that Jesus, God Himself, came to earth to destroy the power of sin, sickness, torment and death.

How do I know for sure that these are the works of the devil? They aren't present in heaven. God does not sponsor sin, sickness, torment or spiritual death. All sin, all sickness, all torment and all spiritual death is from the devil.

We know that God is unalterably opposed to sin, sickness, torment and death because Jesus came to destroy the works of the devil. Jesus' actions reveal the Father's attitudes and purposes because He is the exact representation of the Father. (Hebrews 1:3) We should not expect to see anything in the Kingdom of God which we do not also see in Jesus' life. If Jesus acted to correct or alter circumstances and issues in His life, those circumstances and issues do not exist in the Father's kingdom.

Jesus never turned His back on sickness, torment or spiritual death. Jesus never permits sickness or torment to remain unaddressed. Those ideas are not in the book. Sickness and torment were enemies of Jesus because sickness and torment are enemies of the Father. Jesus went around healing and delivering from torment all who were oppressed by the devil. (Acts 10:38) The things Jesus opposed do not exist in the Father's kingdom.

The Word is clear that death entered the world through the intervention of the devil. Death was accompanied by its ugly step-sisters, sickness and torment. All sin is from the devil. All sickness is from the devil. All torment is from the devil. God does not use the devil's work to accomplish His purposes. I am not saying God will not work in the midst of an attack by the devil. I am saying that God is not the author of the works of the devil and does not use them to punish or discipline His people.

Jesus was manifested to destroy the works of the devil. (1 John 3:8) The last words of Jesus on the cross were: "It is finished." (John 19:30) He did not mean that His life was finished. It was not. Rather, He was announcing that He had finished the work He came to do. We know that He was successful. *"And having disarmed the powers and authorities, he made a public spectacle of them, triumphing over them by the cross."* (Colossians 2:15) Not only did Jesus destroy the works of the devil, He made a public spectacle of them.

Can't you just see a ticker-tape parade down Fifth Avenue in New York City. Jesus is being hailed as the triumphant hero and king. He has all the powers and all the authorities which answered to the devil in cages subject to His total control. Not only are they in those cages, but the world can now see how tiny and insignificant they are when compared to the magnificence of Jesus. They have been brought from darkness where they postured and roared into the light where they are totally defeated.

The result of the devil's defeat is that Jesus "*has made perfect forever those who are being made holy by his one sacrifice.*" (Hebrews 10:14) I am made perfect in my spirit because of what Jesus did, not *because* of any of my actions. I am made perfect *in spite of* my actions. I am progressively being made holy by the transformation made by the renewing of my mind. (Romans 12:2)

Since I have already been made perfect, and my sanctification continues by the renewing of my mind, I should spend precious little time "navel gazing." I have no power or ability to clean up my act sufficiently to enter heaven on my own merits. I can get there solely through what Jesus has already accomplished.

Rather than navel gazing, I should be seeking to co-labor with God in accomplishing His purposes in the kingdom. Paul describes us as "*workers together with Him*" or "*God's fellow workers.*" (2 Corinthians 6:1 KJV and NIV respectively.) The work of God which continues today is two-fold, the spread of the kingdom to new believers and the delivery of God's compassion to those who are in any way afflicted by the devil.

Save His People From Their Sins

The angel of the Lord explained to Joseph that Mary would give birth to a son who was to be named Jesus because "*He will save His people from their sins.*" (Matthew 1:21)

The name Jesus means "Yahweh is our salvation." The English word *salvation* is a translation of the Greek word *soteria*, a derivative of *sozo*. Thus, the very name of Jesus reminds us that God is providing our complete restoration of body, soul and spirit. The very name of Jesus assures us that God Himself would provide the sacrifice needed to atone for the sins of the whole world.

The Greek word translated *save* is *sozo*. *Sozo* implies a complete restoration including body, soul and spirit. The word is huge. It is too limiting to read "save" as fire insurance only. Jesus did not come simply to change my destination from hell to heaven. Yes, He made it possible for me to accept a reservation in heaven and cancel my reservation in hell. He did so much more. He not only got me out of the fire, He gave me life to the full. (John 10:10)

Now that is good news!

Jesus was sent to provide a complete restoration of my body, soul and spirit to the same status mankind enjoyed before the fall. He knew that prior status because God the Son is the agent of creation.

What are the hallmarks of Mankind's status before the fall?

- Man was created in God's own image;
- Man was not sick;
- Man was not subject to torment;
- Man was at peace;
- Man was not controlled by a sinful nature;
- Man was filled with life resulting from God's spirit being breathed into him;
- Man was completely dependent upon God for the knowledge of good and evil; and
- Man stood unashamed in daily communion with God.

Jesus was sent to restore all of these kingdom realities. He rescued us from the dominion of darkness. God brought us into the kingdom of the Son He loves, in whom we have redemption. God has reconciled us by Jesus' death to present us holy in His sight, without blemish and free from accusation. (Colossians 1: 13-22)

That status to which we are restored sounds a lot like Jesus' status as a man. If we have the same status in the kingdom as Jesus, the man, had, those things He did while walking the earth are possible for us, too.

Even though we are holy in His sight, without blemish and free from accusation, scripture is clear that apart from Jesus we can do nothing. (John 15:5) Jesus Himself promised us:

- if He remains in us and we remain in Him we will bear much fruit (John 15:5); and
- if we remain in Jesus and His words remain in us we may *"ask whatever you wish and it will be given to you."* (John 15:7)

This promise comes with a caveat: "*This is to my Father's glory, that you bear much fruit, showing yourselves to be my disciples.*" (John 15:8) The purpose of bearing much fruit is not to enhance our reputation but rather to bring glory to the Father.

Jesus promised us that He was leaving His peace with us. He admonished us not to let our hearts be troubled. We are not to be afraid. (John 15:27) When we are filled with Jesus' peace, our hearts are not troubled and we are not afraid, we are restored to God's image.

To Seek and Save What Was Lost

Zacchaeus was a short, wealthy, tax collector who was so excited about seeing Jesus that he ran around in a crowd and ultimately climbed a tree just to see Him. Jesus told Zacchaeus, "*the Son of Man came to seek and save what was lost.*" (Luke 19:1-10)

Not only did Jesus come to *save (sozo)* what was lost, He came to *seek* what was lost. Jesus is in full time pursuit of those who have not yet believed in Him. What a comfort to those who have family and friends who are not yet found!

Jesus told us that *anyone* who has faith in Him will do those things He had been doing. (John 14:12) Since Jesus is in full-time pursuit of those who have not yet believed in Him, it seems clear that we are called to join in that pursuit.

Jesus' full time pursuit of the lost is illustrated in the parable of the prodigal son. The younger son demanded his portion of his father's estate and then squandered this wealth in wild living. It finally became apparent to him that he had made a serious error. The NIV puts it "When he came to his senses," he purposed to return to his father, confess his sins and ask to be treated as one of the hired men. While he was still a long way off, his "father saw him and was filled with compassion for him; he ran to his son, threw his arms around him and kissed him." (Luke 15:11-32)

The son believed that this material portion of his father's estate would be sufficient to sustain him. He believed a life of independence from his father would be more satisfying. He was wrong! He squandered his inheritance and fell into a season of lack.

During his absence, the father continued to seek the return of his lost son while permitting him to taste the full measure of his selfish desire to live in total independence.

God is like that. While He honors our free will, He is ever searching the horizon, eager to run and greet us, throwing His arms around us when we finally come to our senses, return home (sometimes described as repentance), confess our knowledge of our sin, and ask for a renewed relationship with our Father.

In the parable, the father was filled with compassion for his son. The father undoubtedly knew the consequences of his son's actions, knew the conditions under which his son had been living, and knew that he was, at all times, both willing and able to restore his son to his household and his status as a son. The father's heart was set upon restoration.

The father's compassion in the parable is a minor glimpse of our heavenly Father's compassion for us. The father in the parable accepted the son, restored him and held a celebration.

God is even better than the father of the parable. The father in the parable did not take on the son's condition, walk in his son's environment, and give his life for the forgiveness of the son with only the possibility that the son would come to his senses. Only God would do that!

God was not content to scan the horizon in search of us. He sent Jesus to live as one of us, die as the perfect sacrifice for the payment for our sins, bear our sicknesses and deliver us from torment. He did all this only to put in place an environment in which we could, upon coming to our senses, confess Jesus as Lord and believe that God raised Him from the dead. Our heavenly Father did all of those things long before we were in existence so that, should we ever come to our senses, we would be able to return to the home Adam forfeited. Thank God that Jesus "came to seek and save what was lost."

Bring Us Life to the Full

Jesus explained to the Pharisees: " *The thief comes only to steal and kill and destroy; I have come that they may have life, and have it to the full. I am the good shepherd. The good shepherd lays down his life for the sheep.*" (John 10:10-11) The abundant life Jesus promised results from a complete restoration of body, soul and spirit. This is life to the full. We can receive that life only because our good shepherd laid down His life for us, His sheep.

The thief came to steal, kill and destroy. The devil is a created being, more crafty than any of the wild animals the LORD God had made. (Genesis 3:1) I need to be aware of his craftiness. He uses this craftiness to attack me where I am weakest.

If my knowledge, understanding and appreciation of my relationship to God is weak, I should expect him to try to exploit that weakness. If my knowledge of what God has said is weak, I should expect him to try to exploit that weakness. When I am strong in my knowledge of God's Word and secure in my relationship to the Father in the kingdom, the devil's attacks are easily discerned and avoided. It is when I am weak (all too often) that I am vulnerable to attack.

The serpent encouraged the woman to question the word of God. He approached the woman, in part, because her knowledge of what God had said was second hand. The serpent asked, *"Did God really say . . . ."* The devil questioned God's reliability by questioning the reliability of the source of her information. The only way she would know what God said was to rely on what the man said that God said. Once the source was changed from God to the man, the battle was now being fought on different ground. Once the source was the man, the truth of what he had reported as a conversation from God could be assailed.

The woman knew for certain that it had been *reported to her* that she was not to eat of the fruit of the tree of the knowledge of good and evil or she would surely die. This must have seemed like a harsh pronouncement from a God she knew to be a caring, loving provider, comforter and friend. So what did the serpent do? He suggested a reason why God couldn't have said what he said. He provided her *intellect* a way to doubt the accuracy of what she had heard from the man and a reason why she should not comply. At the devil's suggestion, she saw that the fruit was good for food, pleasing to the eye, and desirable for gaining wisdom. With all these pluses, how could it be that God had said if she ate fruit from this tree that she would surely die? The woman's intellectual inability to understand the wisdom of the one and only command she had received prevented her from relying on the providence of God gained through absolute trust in the truth of His Word. The serpent used her shortcoming and limited understanding as the key to steal, kill and destroy.

Make no mistake. God had told the man that he would surely die if he ate the fruit from the tree in the center of the garden. Although the devil got the woman to question whether God had said that, and if He had, did He mean it, the truth was that eating that fruit would lead to death.

God said death was the consequence of eating of the fruit from the tree of the knowledge of good and evil. The woman and then the man ate it. Their physical bodies did not die for over 800 years following this encounter. Is God a liar? Did Moses get this part wrong? Choose! Either

God is a liar, in which case we need not bother with the rest of the book, or the woman and the man died – not 800 plus years later – right then.

The death experienced by the man and the woman was spiritual death, not physical death. Spiritual death includes loss of being created in the image and likeness of God. No longer were the man and the woman to be free from sickness, disease and torment. No longer were they to be able to live a spirit controlled life. A life controlled by a sin nature began.

Although Adam was created in God's image, Adam's children were created "in his own likeness, in his own image." (Genesis 5:1-4) When these children were born, the man and the woman were already spiritually dead. Adam's children, born in his own likeness and image, were born spiritually dead. All of us born since the fall are born spiritually dead and in need of *sozo*, the complete restoration of body, soul and spirit.

God expelled the man and the woman from the garden. He posted "cherubim and a flaming sword flashing back and forth to guard the way to the tree of life." (Genesis 3:24) Only if the man and woman were spiritually dead would it be necessary to guard the way to the tree of life.

What mankind needs is restoration of the spiritual life lost at the time of the fall. Jesus spoke directly to this issue.

> *For just as the Father raises the dead and gives them life, even so the Son gives life to whom he is pleased to give it. . . . "I tell you the truth, whoever hears my word and believes him who sent me has eternal life and will not be condemned; he has crossed over from death to life. I tell you the truth, a time is coming and has now come when the dead will hear the voice of the Son of God and those who hear will live. (John 5:21-25)*

The aim of salvation is not to make us without sin in our actions. Rather, the aim of salvation is the complete restoration of life.

Jesus died to fulfill the sacrificial requirement of the law for the forgiveness of sins. The shedding of blood in the perfect sacrifice was completed on Friday. What about Sunday? Jesus rose on Sunday and lives forever to give us life in Him.

Unbelief is the sin which can keep us separated from God.

> *"For God did not send his Son into the world to condemn the world, but to save the world through him. Whoever believes in him is not condemned, but whoever does not believe stands condemned already because he has not believed in the name of God's one and only Son." (John 3:17-18)*

Unless we believe in Jesus, we already are condemned. We need not do one more thing to go to hell. No acts of disobedience are required. No bad thoughts or attitudes are necessary. We are already condemned.

This is the essential truth which Paul recognized when he said: *"Therefore, there is now no condemnation for those who are in Christ Jesus, because through Christ Jesus the law of the Spirit of life set me free from the law of sin and death."* (Romans 8:1-2)

Under the law of sin and death, the wages of sin is death. However, under the law of the Spirit of life, the gift of God is eternal life in Christ Jesus our Lord. (Romans 6:23) Death is payment for our sin of unbelief. We receive eternal life in Jesus as a gift. If we have to work for it, it is not a gift.

Jesus came to give us back the life which the liar had stolen and destroyed. The really good news is that the life He came to give us is life to the full, the abundant life. This abundant life includes not only forgiveness of sin but also physical healing and delivery from torment.

To Preach the Good News

Jesus came not only to do the flashy stuff of healing and casting out demons, he came to preach the good news of the Kingdom. The fourth chapter of the Gospel of Luke reports that Jesus put on quite a display in Capernaum. The people were impressed with His teaching, and then the fun started. The general awe which started from His teaching with authority now was fanned into a flame by His ordering an evil spirit to depart. A demon recognized him and announced Jesus was the Holy One of God. He even suggested that Jesus had come to destroy him. Jesus sternly rebuked him and ordered him to leave the afflicted man.

While the news about Jesus was getting around (and don't you know it was quick), Jesus went to Simon Peter's house and quickly healed Peter's mother-in-law with little or no fanfare. By sundown, things were out of hand. All in the vicinity who had various kinds of diseases were brought to Jesus. He laid his hands on each one and they were healed – all of them! While *all* were healed, demons came out of *many*, each one announcing "You are the Son of God." Although Jesus rebuked them and commanded them to be quiet, the place was abuzz.

Early the following morning, as Jesus went out to a solitary place, the people were already looking for Him, purposed to keep Him from leaving them. Jesus declined the invitation to stay explaining, *"I must preach the good news of the kingdom of God to the other towns also, because that is why I was sent."* (Luke 4:43)

Jesus knew there was more to His mission. He knew the compassion of God would not be fulfilled simply by healing of those afflicted in one geographical location. The compassion of God carried with it an imperative that the restoration of life be offered to all men.

Consider the Great Commission: *"Go into all the world and preach the good news to all creation. Whoever believes and is baptized will be saved, but whoever does not believe will be condemned."* (Mark 16:15-16) Jesus knew that the Father's will was that none would perish but that everyone would come to repentance. (2 Pet 3:9) The same idea is reflected in the most memorized scripture from the Bible: *"For God so loved the world that he gave his one and only Son, that whoever believes in him shall not perish but have eternal life.* (John 3:16)

This very idea is represented in the following:

> *"Everyone who calls on the name of the Lord will be saved." How, then, can they call on the one they have not believed in? And how can they believe in the one of whom they have not heard? And how can they hear without someone preaching to them? And how can they preach unless they are sent? . . . Consequently, faith comes from hearing the message, and the message is heard through the word of Christ."* (Romans 10:13-17)

It was important to Jesus that as many as possible hear the message. He knew that faith comes from hearing the message. Jesus' words are the "word of Christ." Jesus came to present the message as often as possible to as many as possible so that faith could take hold.

Jesus had the full backing of heaven to accomplish his purpose. When we join Jesus in pursuing the same goals for which He was sent, we also have the backing of heaven to accomplish those goals. *"As the Father has sent me, I am sending you."* (John 20:21)

CHAPTER SEVEN

Spiritual Gifts

The realization that Jesus the man relied exclusively on the power of the Holy Spirit to perform all miracles, signs and wonders was huge in changing our way of thinking. Hard on the heels of that realization in the rank of importance was an understanding that the Holy Spirit whose power performed all Jesus' miracles is the same Holy Spirit who resides in me and whose power is available to me through Baptism with the Holy Spirit. He has lost none of His power, He is able to do now what He did then.

Since God does not change, the things the Father was doing then He is doing now. Since I have the same standing before God because of the atonement that Jesus the man enjoyed, I can legitimately expect the Holy Spirit to be just as willing and able to heal today when I ask as He was in Jesus' time.

The Holy Spirit seems to make some believers nervous. This unfamiliarity arises from bad teaching and lack of experience. It is helpful to recall that the Holy Spirit is none other than God Himself. He is no more scary than Jesus or God the Father. He just hasn't been discussed positively in some polite circles. Nonetheless, He is an old friend who is always on our side and up to nothing but good for each of us.

It makes no sense whatsoever to say, "I believe in God the Father and Jesus, His one and only Son but I am not so sure about that Holy Spirit guy. He scares me."

It is helpful to remind yourself that the Holy Spirit is a person not an unknown force that is somewhat out of control.

The Holy Spirit has not "retired." He did not become tired at the end of the Apostolic Age and check into heaven's Old Folks Home. He is active in the world today as He resides in us. Appendix One deals with arguments propounded by some cessationists concerning the on-going action of the Holy Spirit. Nancy and I can testify with certainty that the Holy Spirit is working continually in the world today – and with great power.

The Holy Spirit who resides in me is the same Holy Spirit who worked through Jesus. Believers receive life by the indwelling of the Holy Spirit at the time of salvation. It is His life that Jesus imparts to us when we "*cross over from death to life.*" (John 5:24) He is *in* all believers. The Holy Spirit is *in* us for our benefit.

Just as Jesus received power at His baptism with the Holy Spirit following John's baptism, The Holy Spirit is *upon us* after our baptism with the Holy Spirit. He is *upon us* for the benefit of others.

The Holy Spirit who is upon us has all the same power He had when He was upon Jesus. We do not receive Holy Spirit, Jr. We do not receive Holy Spirit, Lite. The indwelling power of the Holy Spirit includes the fullness of the power of God. I may not be strong. He is omnipotent.

The Apostle Paul explained spiritual gifts to the church at Corinth.

> *Now about spiritual gifts, brothers, I do not want you to be ignorant. . . . There are different kinds of gifts, but the same Spirit. There are different kinds of service, but the same Lord. There are different kinds of working, but the same God works all of them in all men. Now to each one the manifestation of the Spirit is given for the common good.* (1 Corinthians 12:1-7)

Spiritual Life and Manifestation

There is a difference between the indwelling of the Holy Spirit giving us His life and a manifestation of the Holy Spirit. The Greek word translated "manifestation" is *phanerosis* which means an exhibition or expression. The root word in Greek is *phaneroo* which means to render apparent or show oneself. Many believers are indwelt by the Holy Spirit but there is no manifestation of the Holy Spirit in their lives. That is, the Holy Spirit is *in* them but not *upon* them.

Manifestation is different from *fruit*. We are familiar with the fruit of the Holy Spirit.

> *But the fruit of the Spirit is love, joy, peace, patience, kindness, goodness, faithfulness, gentleness and self-control.* (Galatians 5:22-23)

Fruit is what grows on the branch. You can recognize the vine by the type of fruit growing on the branch. However, the fruit is not a manifestation of the power residing in the vine. Fruit is a result of the power of the vine.

Paul tells us that a manifestation of the Spirit is given to each of us. Baptism in the Holy Spirit puts a sure and certain *phanerosis* within reach of every believer.

The manifestation is not given for our amusement. Rather, the manifestation is given for the common good. If the gift does not serve the common good, it is not a *phanerosis* of the Holy Spirit. If the outflow in my life is not directed to the common good, it isn't the Holy Spirit that is outflowing.

Peter explained to Cornelius that after Jesus was anointed by God with the Holy Spirit and with power He went around doing good. (Acts 10:38) The Greek word translated "good" means a philanthropic act. When Jesus was "doing good" He was letting the Holy Spirit flow through Him, not performing morally upright acts. A philanthropist is one who gives away his treasure. That is exactly what Jesus was doing. It is likewise what we are called to do.

I am not suggesting Jesus' acts were not morally upright. Rather, I am suggesting that moral rectitude was not the hallmark of the "good" that Jesus was doing. He gave away all that the Holy Spirit had given Him by doing what He saw the Father do and saying only what He heard the Father say. All of this power was directed toward destroying the works of the devil. (1 John 3:8)

Paul makes it clear that the different gifts, the different service and the different works are all the product of the same God working in men. In each instance, it is God working, not man.

Paul then proceeds to list nine gifts of the Holy Spirit.

- Word of wisdom;
- Word of knowledge;
- Faith;
- Gifts of healing;
- Miraculous powers;

- Prophecy;
- Distinguishing between spirits;
- Speaking in different tongues; and
- Interpretation of tongues.

All of these gifts "are the work of one and the same Spirit." (1 Corinthians 12:11) When the Body of Christ is assembled, these manifestations of the Holy Spirit are distributed among the Body as God determines. We do not determine through whom the manifestation will be given. A manifestation is available because God is always working. (John 5:17) We don't always know through whom God will choose to act at any occasion.

When I was baptized with the Holy Spirit in the late 1970's I became increasingly aware of manifestations of the Holy Spirit in my life. My faith simply sky-rocketed, and the increase seemed unrelated to anything I had done or was doing. I just knew that there was a new-found confidence in my relationship with God and His benevolent attitude toward me.

Words of knowledge, words of wisdom and discerning between spirits were somewhat surprising gifts because they appeared with no rational basis and no relation to particular circumstances which might be interpreted to have given rise to a thought or idea. Instead, all of a sudden, the idea or knowledge was available, fully formed. It didn't require any further input from me.

I learned early on that I could not increase the occurrence of these gifts nor demand that I know things for my sole benefit. I might receive some direction for my life as an answer to prayer but true words of knowledge and wisdom appeared irrespective of my will and outside my control.

I struggled mightily with tongues. Finally I understood that unless the Holy Spirit was speaking, there would be no utterance in tongues. I also learned that unless I provided my tongue, nothing would be forced from my mouth.

My experience with knowledge, wisdom, tongues and discerning between spirits did not prepare me to properly apprehend the gifts of healing or miraculous powers. When it came to gifts of healing and miraculous powers, for reasons I do not understand, I believed that if I had either of those gifts, I would know it and be changed by it. I expected one who had the gifts of healing to feel empowered in a personal sense. I further expected that one with the gifts of healing would be able to bring healings into existence by the power given him.

It doesn't make sense that I could fully understand that I could not "gin up" a word of knowledge or a word of wisdom but still believed that one who had received a gift of healing would be able to produce healing upon demand. I knew I didn't feel empowered in relation to knowledge and wisdom. It simply came when it came. Why in the world, then, would I have a different expectation when it came to a gift of healing.

When I am confused, it helps to go back to the Owner's Manual, the Bible. Since all spiritual gifts are manifestations of the Holy Spirit, it is always the Holy Spirit who is acting, not the individual. I could easily accept that I could not "know" the unlearned and unlearnable. Rather, the Holy Spirit knew and would share that knowledge with me for the benefit of others. Somehow I was confused about healing. I just didn't see it as simple as it is. All healings, all miracles, all signs and all wonders are done directly by God and God alone and are manifestations of His presence here with us. God manifests Himself among us for His glory, not for ours.

I was helped significantly in my limited understanding of this gift of healing when I read an article by A. B. Simpson (1843-1919). Simpson was the founder of the Christian and Missionary Alliance, wrote more than seventy books on the Bible and the Christian way of life. In an article entitled "*Himself*" A. B. Simpson wrote:

> *I often hear people say, 'I wish I could get hold of Divine Healing, but I cannot.' Sometimes they say, "I have got it.' If I ask them, "What have you got?" the answer is sometimes, I've got the blessing; I have got the theory; I have got the healing; and sometimes I have got the sanctification.*

> *But I thank God that we have been taught that it is not the blessing, it is not the healing, it is not the sanctification, it is not the thing, it is not the it that you want, but it is something better. It is 'the Christ'; it is Himself. . . .*

> *It is the person of Jesus Christ we want.*

> *At last He said to me – Oh so tenderly – 'My child, just take Me, and let Me be in you the constant supply of all this, Myself."*

Jesus knew that by Himself He could do nothing. (John 5:19) He was careful to say only what He heard the Father saying and to say it just as

He was instructed. (John 12:49) He waited for the power of the Lord to be present to heal. (Luke 5:17)

Even after God anointed Jesus of Nazareth with the Holy Spirit and with power, he could do nothing by Himself, He said nothing on His own accord, and He didn't have the power to heal. He relied totally upon the power of the Holy Spirit to manifest the presence and power of God. He awaited the *phanerosis* of the Holy Spirit.

When we realize that the healing power resides in Jesus, Himself, and that we have nothing in us to add, the pressure for healing and miraculous signs evaporates. If Jesus does the healing , the person gets healed. If Jesus does not heal, there is no healing. It certainly is not going to come from me.

The Purpose of Signs

Signs provide a direction to a greater reality than the sign itself. I cannot exit through an exit sign. Rather, I use the exit sign to find the location of the exit door. If a sign doesn't point the way to a greater reality, it is useless. There is no purpose in the zing and the zang of signs unless the zing and the zang point to God's presence and power. Miracles, signs and wonders will never point to a human being. They only point to Jesus, Himself.

It's Not Me

The full panoply of spiritual gifts may well not be known to man. I am certain that the spiritual gifts we know about which manifest the Holy Spirit for the common good are available to the Body of Christ. In each instance, it is God who works all of them in all men. It just isn't me. It never is. It is always Him.

Since it is never me, I can be certain that the healer is God Himself. If I cannot "do it" myself, likely I cannot mess it up either.

Since I am not "doing it" I can have absolute assurance that if you do what I have been doing, you will not be "doing it" either.

CHAPTER EIGHT

Take Jesus At His Word

I confess that prior to 2008 I read around the largest and best promises in the Bible. I read the promises. I prayed for results that I did not perceive to have appeared. The disappointment of experiences apparently contrary to the Word of God gave birth to imaginations and denials of the truth of the Word. Oh, I knew the Word was true, it was just more true for others than it was for me.

Nancy and I feel that we almost stepped into a parallel universe in 2008 and have stayed there ever since. For reasons that we do not fully comprehend, we began to participate in miracles, signs and wonders at an ever increasing rate. In our life now, we expect that God will miraculously intervene in the circumstances of those around us on a regular basis. The occurrence of miraculous healings seems to be the rule rather than the exception. We are seeing God deliver his compassion by miraculous healings and delivery from torment in the usual course of praying for the sick and tormented.

We believe that one of the reasons for this change is that we began taking God at His word. The Gospel of John contains an account of a man who took Jesus at His word. His history changed as a result. Our history and the history of those around us changed dramatically once we began taking Jesus at His word. We now better understand why Smith Wigglesworth delighted in saying, "Only believe."

There was a certain royal official whose son in Capernaum was sick and close to dead. (John 4:46-54) This official was not a member of any tribe of Israel but rather was most likely an official in Herod's court in Capernaum. Even though he was not a Jew, he had heard about Jesus, perhaps through the reports of Jesus' turning the water into wine at the wedding feast in Cana.

When Jesus returned to Cana for the first time after this wedding miracle, the royal official went to Jesus and begged Him to come to his home and heal his son. The official showed either a lot of faith in Jesus or the desperation of his situation when he sought out a Jew for healing. He would have known that, according to Jewish law, Jesus would have little, if anything, to do with a gentile. He certainly would not be expected to visit the home of a gentile, regardless of the reason. Upon arrival at Cornelius' house, Peter said, *"You are well aware that it is against our law for a Jew to associate with a Gentile or visit him."* (Acts 10:28) The royal official was asking Jesus to violate the law by associating with him and going to his home to heal his son.

Jesus seems to have mildly rebuked the official, saying *"Unless you people see miraculous signs and wonders, you will never believe."* (John 4:48) It is not clear whether Jesus was specifically addressing the official or a crowd of Galileans. Perhaps he was referring to the lack of faith He had noticed in his home town. (Matthew 13:58) In any event, it is clear that the official already believed. He sought out Jesus and begged Him to come to his home and heal his son.

If the rebuke was directed at the official, he was undeterred. He said, *"Sir, come down before my child dies."* (John 4:49)

Jesus did not directly refuse to go to the official's home, but said, *"You may go. Your son will live."* (John 4:50) Jesus dismissed the official with the promise his son would live. There is no report that Jesus laid hands on the official who was standing in the gap for his son. There is no report that Jesus prayed for the son's healing. He simply promised the official that his son would live.

The official's response to this promise was extraordinary. He did not plead and beg Jesus to come and heal his son in the same manner He had healed others. Because Jesus offered no touch, no prayer, no word of encouragement, no exhortation to the son to recover, and did not command any evil spirit to come out of the son, the official could have been easily excused if he had tried to convince Jesus his son was worthy of healing. The official could have been easily excused if he had insisted that Jesus at least come into his son's presence and *do something*. It would be understandable if he had asked Jesus for an anointed prescription or specific instructions of what the son should do to regain his health.

The official did none of those things. Rather, the official "took Jesus at his word and departed." (John 4:50) Now, that is a demonstration of complete faith in Jesus. In essence he said, "Jesus said it, I believe it and that settles it." He was not going home to heal his son. He was going home because he had been *promised* by the person God had anointed with the Holy Spirit and with power that there was nothing more required. It was done when Jesus said, "your son will live." God's word had completed its purpose when Jesus said it. The royal official knew his son would live *because Jesus said so.*

While he was still on his way home, the official learned that his son was living. He didn't ask how his son started on the road to recovery. He didn't ask whether anyone at his home had taken any heroic steps. He didn't ask about any prayers for healing. He simply asked when the healing manifested in his son's body.

When he learned that the fever had left the boy at the same time that Jesus promised his recovery, he reported that occurrence to his household. The result was that "*he and all his household believed.*" (John 4:53)

We changed our way of thinking in 2008 and since that time we have endeavored the best we can to believe that it is true that:

- Jesus was manifested to destroy the works of the devil (1 John 3:8);
- Jesus' atoning sacrifice was completely sufficient for forgiveness of sin, physical healing and delivery from torment (Isaiah 53:4-5);
- God anointed Jesus of Nazareth with the Holy Spirit and with power (Acts 10:38);
- Jesus went around doing good, healing all who were oppressed by the devil, because God was with Him (Acts 10:38);
- Jesus acted in the power of the Holy Spirit because He could do only what He saw his Father do (John 5:19);
- Jesus spoke in the power of the Holy Spirit because He said only what He heard the Father say (John 8:28; John 12:50);
- Whoever hears Jesus' word and believes Him who sent Jesus has eternal life and will not be condemned; he has crossed over from death to life (John 5:24);
- Jesus sent us just as the Father had sent Him (John 20:21);

- We have received power from on high in the baptism of the Holy Spirit (Luke 24:49; Acts 1:4-8);

- Anyone who has faith in Jesus will do what He did, and even greater things than these, because Jesus went to the Father (John 14:12); and

- Jesus will do whatever we ask in His name, so that the Son may bring glory to the Father; we may ask Him for anything in His name, and He will do it (John 14:13).

No longer do we read these promises out of scripture. No longer do we read around these promises, supposing they are for others but not for us. Rather, we take Jesus at His word. Everything has changed!

CHAPTER NINE

Paradigm Shift

Jesus announced a paradigm shift had occurred in the heavenly realms.

> *"The Law and the Prophets were proclaimed until John. Since that time, the good news of the kingdom of God is being preached, and everyone is forcing his way into it."* (Luke 16:16) (NIV)

> *"The law and the prophets were until John: since that time the kingdom of God is preached, and every man presseth into it."* (Luke 16:16) (KJV)

Something was dramatically different before John and after John. Apparently the proclamation of the Law and the Prophets was significantly different from good news of the kingdom of God.

After four hundred years of silence from heaven, God sent the angel Gabriel to John's father, Zechariah, to announce the forthcoming birth of John the Baptist. Gabriel informed Zechariah that John would:

- be filled with the Holy Spirit, even from birth;
- go on before the Lord, in the spirit and power of Elijah;
- turn the hearts of the fathers to their children;
- turn the disobedient to the wisdom of the righteous; and
- make ready a people prepared for the Lord. (Luke 1:11-19)

Six months later, Gabriel appeared to Mary and announced:

> *"You will be with child and give birth to a son, and you are to give him the name Jesus. He will be great and will be called the Son of the Most High. The Lord God will give him the throne of his father David, and he will reign over the house of Jacob forever; his kingdom will never end."* (Luke 1:31-33)

Three months after Gabriel's visit to Mary, John was born to her cousin, Elizabeth. At that time, Zechariah prophesied that John would:

- be called a prophet of the Most High;
- go on before the Lord to prepare the way for him; and
- give people the knowledge of salvation through the forgiveness of sins, because of the tender mercy of our God. (Luke 1:67-79)

The beginning of this paradigm shift began with John's public ministry. Paul described the change brought by the paradigm shift.

> *There is now no condemnation for those who are in Christ Jesus, because through Christ Jesus the law of the Spirit of life set me free from the law of sin and death.* (Romans 8:1)

The *law of sin and death* governed until John. After John, the *law of the Spirit of life* was available to believers for the first time.

Paul clearly recognized the law of sin and death as an inferior reality to the law of the Spirit of life. The law of sin and death was weakened by our sinful nature.

> *For what the law was powerless to do in that it was weakened by the sinful nature, God did by sending his own Son in the likeness of sinful man to be a sin offering. And so he condemned sin in sinful man, in order that the righteous requirements of the law might be fully met in us, who do not live according to the sinful nature but according to the Spirit.* (Romans 8:2-4)

I am incapable of satisfying the voracious appetite of the law. God sent his own Son to become a sin offering to satisfy the requirements of the law. That sin offering paid the penalty for my sins *in full*.

Since all of my sins were in the future as of the time of Jesus' sacrifice, His death on the cross needed to be sufficient to forgive whatever sins my future might bring. The penalty necessary for forgiveness of my sins was paid in full by Jesus' death. He thought of it all. Nothing more was required.

John the Baptist and Jesus both shared the prophecy announcing this paradigm shift. They both proclaimed that "the kingdom of heaven is near" (Matthew 3:2; 4:17) or the "kingdom of God is near" (Mark 1:14).

John the Baptist and Jesus announced a new life available to believers:

John: *"Whoever believes in the Son has eternal life, but whoever rejects the Son will not see life, for God's wrath remains on him."* (John 3:36)

Jesus: *"I tell you the truth, whoever hears my word and believes him who sent me has eternal life and will not be condemned; he has crossed over from death to life.* (John 5:24)

"For God so loved the world that he gave his one and only Son, that whoever believes in him shall not perish but have eternal life. For God did not send his Son into the world to condemn the world, but to save the world through him. Whoever believes in him is not condemned, but whoever does not believe stands condemned already because he has not believed in the name of God's one and only Son." (John 3:16-18)

The message of the kingdom of God is clear. Until we believe in Jesus, we are dead in our sins. God's wrath remains on us. Crossing over from death to life is the beginning of entry into the kingdom of God.

The kingdom of God did not come to equip us to never sin again. In the kingdom, our righteousness is not dependent upon living a sinless life. Rather, the kingdom of God came so that we would be afforded the opportunity to become alive by belief in Jesus.

Yet to all who received him, to those who believed in his name, he gave the right to become children of God — children born not of natural descent, nor of human decision or a husband's will, but born of God. (John 1:12-13)

To enter the kingdom of God and receive the gift of eternal life, I must believe in Jesus. When I enter the kingdom of God, I:

- was born from above;
- became free from the law of sin and death; and
- will not be condemned because of the law of the Spirit of life.

Before the coming of the kingdom of God, God acted and man responded, sometimes with supernatural strength and power given by God for a particular occasion. When we enter the kingdom of God, we have this enormous promise:

> *"I tell you the truth, anyone who has faith in me will do what I have been doing. He will do even greater things than these, because I am going to the Father. And I will do whatever you ask in my name, so that the Son may bring glory to the Father. You may ask me for anything in my name, and I will do it."* (John 14:12-14)

The paradigm shift brought the backing of heaven for us to be co-laborers with God to accomplish His purposes. (1 Corinthians 3:9) God would not risk his reputation by charging me to do something without giving me both

- the authority to act on His behalf; and
- access to the power necessary to accomplish His purposes.

Unless I have both the authority to act on His behalf and access to the power necessary, I cannot take Jesus at His word that I will do those things He had been doing, and greater things than those.

Many new truths apply in the kingdom of God.

- Jesus acted once for all.
- Jesus was sacrificed for our sins once for all when he offered himself. (Hebrews 7:27)
- Jesus appeared once for all at the end of the ages to do away with sin by the sacrifice of himself. Christ was sacrificed once to take away the sins of many people. (Hebrews 9:25-28)
- We have been made holy through the sacrifice of the body of Jesus Christ once for all. (Hebrews 10:10).
- My status is completely different in the kingdom.
- If anyone is in Christ, he is a new creation; the old has gone, the new has come. (2 Cor. 5:17)
- We are God's workmanship, created in Christ Jesus to do good works, which God prepared in advance for us to do. (Ephesians 2:10)

- The blood of Christ, cleansed our consciences from acts that lead to death, so that we may serve the living God. (Hebrews 9:14)

- I am free from the power of sin.

- Sin shall not be your master, because you are not under law, but under grace. You have been set free from sin and have become slaves to righteousness. (Romans 6:14-18)

- Christ is the mediator of a new covenant now that He has died as a ransom to set us free from the sins committed under the first covenant. (Hebrews 9:15)

- We are no longer under the supervision of the law. (Galatians 3:25)

- God does not count my sins against me any longer.

- God reconciled the world to Himself in Christ, not counting men's sins against them. (2 Cor. 5:19)

- God forgives my wickedness and will remember my sins no more. (Hebrews 8:12)

- Their sins and lawless acts God will remember no more. Where these have been forgiven, there is no longer any sacrifice for sin. (Hebrews 10:17-18)

- I have been made the righteousness of God.

- God made him who had no sin to be sin for us, so that in him we might become the righteousness of God. (2 Cor. 5:21)

- By one sacrifice Jesus made perfect forever those who are being made holy. (Hebrews 10:14)

- Secrets of the kingdom are unveiled to residents of the kingdom.

- "The secret of the kingdom of God has been given to you. But to those on the outside everything is said in parables so that,"'they may be ever seeing but never perceiving, and ever hearing but never understanding; otherwise they might turn and be forgiven!'" (Mark 4:11-12)

- "The knowledge of the secrets of the kingdom of God has been given to you, but to others I speak in parables, so that, 'though seeing, they may not see; though hearing, they may not understand.'" (Luke 8:10)

- The kingdom of God is not primarily concerned with behavior.
- For the kingdom of God is not a matter of eating and drinking, but of righteousness, peace and joy in the Holy Spirit. (Romans 14:17)
- God manifests His power in the kingdom.
- For the kingdom of God is not a matter of talk but of power. (1 Corinthians 4:20)
- Entry into the kingdom is only possible through God's action, not man's.
- Jesus said again, "Children, how hard it is to enter the kingdom of God! . . . The disciples were even more amazed, and said to each other, "Who then can be saved?" Jesus looked at them and said, "With man this is impossible, but not with God; all things are possible with God." (Mark 10:23-27)

Under the Law and the Prophets, we had neither the job, the power nor the authority to participate in the miracles, signs and wonders God was doing. In the kingdom of God, we are commissioned to co-labor with God in accomplishing His purposes. In order to equip us for that labor, we have been given both the authority to act and access to the power necessary. The paradigm shift described in this chapter opens the door to participation with God in delivering God's compassion to His people.

CHAPTER TEN

Co-Laboring With God

I have some really good news. In all things, God is in charge and we are not.

We get to participate in miracles, signs and wonders as a fellow worker with God but He always has the laboring oar. The concept of "*God's fellow workers*" or "*workers together with God*" (2 Corinthians 6:1) contains an important relational truth. God is the worker, we are the fellow workers. We work together with God. He doesn't work together with us.

Nancy and I began to participate in miracles, signs and wonders when we stopped asking God to bless what we were doing and sought to determine what God was blessing and participate in that. It is His agenda, not ours.

We come to Jesus to receive our rest. He does not come to us to receive His rest. We take His yoke upon us. He does not take our yoke upon Him. If we remember who is in charge, then we are properly yoked.

> *"Take my yoke upon you and learn from me, for I am gentle and humble in heart, and you will find rest for your souls. For my yoke is easy and my burden is light."* (Matthew 11:29-30)

Now, that's the way I want to work. What could be better than to be coupled with a much stronger partner who is both gentle and humble and who will let me rest? If I am going to be yoked, I need that yoke to be easy.

A Matter of Positioning

God is an expert at *positioning* us so that we may participate in His miraculous interventions in history. Consider the Aramean siege of the nation of Israel in the walled city of Samaria. Let's identify the players.

Joram, a son of Ahab became king of Israel in the northern kingdom, which consisted of ten tribes. Joram's capitol city was the walled city of Samaria. He got rid of the stone of Baal which Ahab had made but he clung to the sins of Jeroboam.

Elisha was a significant prophet. He had no use for Joram whatsoever. (2 Kings 3:14) Elisha had a prior history of participating in miracles, including raising the Shunnamite's son from the dead (2 Kings 4:31-36) and healing Naaman of leprosy. (2 Kings 5:1-15)

Naaman was the commander of the Aramean army. He was healed of his leprosy when he reluctantly followed Elisha's instructions to dip himself in the Jordan seven times.

Ben Haddad was the king of Aram. He had continuing controversies with Joram and the nation of Israel. He had previously sent some of his army to capture Elisha in an attempt which failed completely.

God was using the circumstances and the personalities of both Joram and Elisha to demonstrate to Israel that its security came from Him and not from either Elisha or Joram. In the midst of those circumstances, Ben Haddad sent his entire army, commanded by Naaman, to lay siege to the walled city of Samaria.

The siege continued for such a long time that famine was quite severe within the city. The famine got so bad that two women made a pact to kill and eat their babies. After the first baby was eaten, the second mother reneged and hid her child. Joram received the complaint of the second woman while he was walking the walls of the city. His immediate response was anger toward Elisha, apparently believing this bad fortune for the nation of Israel was part of the on-going battle between the two in which Elisha kept getting the upper hand.

In the midst of the famine and hidden baby problem, Elisha prophesied:

> *"Hear the word of the LORD. This is what the LORD says: About this time tomorrow, a seah of flour will sell for a shekel and two seahs of barley for a shekel at the gate of Samaria."*
> (2 Kings 7:1)

This prophecy was met with complete skepticism.

Sitting outside the walled city of Samaria were four lepers. Because of their leprosy, they were unclean and completely unwelcome in Samaria. As part of the besieged nation of Israel, they had no food either.

The same day that Elisha prophesied the coming abundance of food, the lepers had an interesting conversation.

> *And there were four leprous men at the entering in of the gate: and they said one to another, "Why sit we here until we die? If we say, 'We will enter into the city,' then the famine is in the city, and we shall die there: and if we sit still here, we die also. Now therefore come, and let us fall unto the host of the Syrians: if they save us alive, we shall live; and if they kill us, we shall but die."* (2 Kings 7:3-4 KJV)

These lepers asked the critical question for all believers. Once saved, what am I to do? Is there a purpose for me or do I just sit here until I die? *"Why sit we here until we die?"*

The lepers decided on that occasion, not a day before or day later, to go to the camp of the Aramean army. While they were on the way, and totally unbeknownst to them, God performed a miracle that rescued the entire nation of Israel.

> *"The Lord . . . caused the Arameans to hear the sound of chariots and horses and a great army, so that they said to one another, "Look, the king of Israel has hired the Hittite and Egyptian kings to attack us!" So they got up and fled in the dusk and abandoned their tents and their horses and donkeys. They left the camp as it was and ran for their lives."* (2 Kings 7:6-7)

The food and provisions which the army left behind blessed the entire nation of Israel and saved countless lives.

Ask yourself:

- Who performed the miracle?
- Who participated in the miracle?
- What part did each play?
- Who got the glory?

God alone caused the Aramean army to hear chariots and horses and a great army. Significantly, neither the lepers nor any of the residents of the walled city of Samaria heard those chariots and horses. The reason is simple – the army did not exist in the physical realm!

Elisha cannot be credited for the miracle. Elisha did nothing except repeat what he heard God saying. He did absolutely nothing to bring this result to pass. He did not call the nation of Israel to prayer or take any action.

Joram cannot be credited for the miracle. Joram did nothing except threaten to kill Elisha. He did not even call out to God for help.

Naaman cannot be credited for the miracle. Naaman stood in awe of God because he had experienced the power of God in his healing from leprosy. Naaman knew that his army was laying siege to a nation that was blessed by God Himself. When Naaman and his soldiers heard the sounds, he believed that God was on the move.

The lepers cannot be credited for the miracle. God prompted the four lepers to get up at that time to approach the enemy camp. This act was suicidal at best, yet they went. Had they not gone, when would the nation of Israel have learned that God was blessing them with abundance?

God did not perform this miracle because of:

- Elisha's actions as a prophet over a prolonged period;
- Joram's actions as king of Israel;
- a desire to punish Naaman or Ben Haddad;
- any "righteousness" of the lepers; or
- anyone in the circumstance was good.

God performed this miracle for the same reason He performs them all. God performs miracles because He is good and He loves His people. He was not rewarding anyone for good actions. The people of Israel were killing and eating their children. The government was at odds with the church. Distrust and destructive behavior was rampant. They weren't good. He was.

Each of the participants in this event participated in a miracle. No one realized God was performing a miraculous intervention in Israel's history and pouring out His compassion on His people while it was happening. The realization of the truth awaited a report from the unclean and unwelcome lepers of the blessings now available to God's people.

God did it all. No one did anything more than be where God positioned them and report what he saw and heard. The religious followers of Elisha (and Elisha himself) were unable to deliver God's compassion to His people. The existing government, Joram and his army could do nothing other than permit the blessing to be received. Most likely, the ones who reported the blessing were still not permitted within the city because the leprosy persisted.

God did it all, from beginning to end. He acted in the history of His people to demonstrate his compassion and His love. No one prayed to God to change His mind. God was not rewarding the faith of anyone involved in the circumstances.

Each of the lepers was a fellow worker with God. He didn't help them perform the miracle. The miracle was not a product of power He granted to them. Rather, He positioned them in a way to observe and report what He was doing.

Elisha was a fellow worker with God. God didn't help Elisha accomplish any result. Elisha was positioned in a way to speak God's word to the people so that when the miracle was discovered the following day all the glory would be given to God.

All the co-laboring followed God's plan, not man's plan. What could be easier than simply being in the right place, positioned by God, and doing what God prompts you to do when He prompts you to do it? Had the lepers jumped the gun, they likely would have been killed. Instead, God prompted them to take their halting steps in pursuit of His purposes.

The lepers were not experts in delivering God's compassion to His people. Yet, they were used mightily by God to accomplish His purposes.

Miraculous healings today are accomplished in exactly the same fashion. Someone may have a word of knowledge that God is going to heal a particular person or a particular condition. However, that knowledge does not enable the person in his own power to heal anyone. The person being healed may feel something and recognize the power of God is upon him, or he may not. The confirmation of many miraculous healings awaits a sensory perception of a change that cannot be explained in any other way than an act of God.

CHAPTER ELEVEN

Do What Jesus Did

Jesus' Extraordinary Promise

I tell you the truth, anyone who has faith in me will do what I have been doing. He will do even greater things than these, because I am going to the Father. And I will do whatever you ask in my name, so that the Son may bring glory to the Father. You may ask me for anything in my name, and I will do it. (John 14:12-14)

Jesus promised I will do those things He had been doing. That promise is conditioned only upon having faith in Jesus. The NIV translation of the Greek is *anyone who has faith in me*. The King James translation is *he that believeth on me*. All believers are included.

The excluding factor is failure to have *faith in* or *believe on* Jesus. Absent that faith or belief, the promise does not apply. The qualification is simply have *faith in* or *believe on* Jesus. If you have faith in Jesus or believe on Jesus, you are included. Once you are qualified, you are qualified. Jesus said so.

Jesus did not say I *can do* those things He had been doing but rather that I *will do* those things. Nothing the Bible tells me I should do is possible in my own power. Apart from Jesus I can do nothing. (John 15:5)

If I *will do* certain things, there must be an authorization for me to access the power necessary to perform the tasks. Jesus did not say that I *will* participate in things in the kingdom only to withhold access to the power to get those things done. I *will do* those things Jesus had been doing *only* in communion with Him.

Jesus could only do what He saw the Father doing. (John 5:19) If I am going to do the things Jesus did, I will need to know what the Father is doing. Miraculous healing will never be my province. It shall remain the province of the Father who determines who, when and how.

In order to heal the sick, Jesus had to ascertain whether the power of the Lord was present and what the Father was healing at that time. He also needed to know whether the power to heal was to be applied to all who were there or only to a select few. Thinking about these issues furnishes valuable insight into Jesus' prayers.

We know that *"Jesus often withdrew to lonely places and prayed."* (Luke 5:16) What do you suppose He was praying about? He did not spend one split second on confessing his sins – He had none. He likely did not pray for his daily bread. After all, He knew how to take what was available, give thanks for it, and then watch as the Father increased the supply to fill the need. Isn't that exactly what He did at the wedding feast in Cana? (John 2:1-10) Isn't that exactly what He did at the feeding of the five thousand and the four thousand? (Matthew 14:15-21; Matthew 15:32-28)

Jesus must have prayed to learn *where* the Father was acting, *upon whom* the Father would be pouring out His compassion, and *what* was the nature of the problem. Scripture records only one person being healed beside the pool at Bethesda. There may have been others healed that day. Or, there may not! Jesus needed to know which man occupied God's attention for healing that day. Jesus likewise needed to know whether the Father was only healing that day or was He also teaching, preaching or delivering from torment.

Consider the raising of Lazarus. (John 11:1-44) There was a delay of three or four days from the time that Jesus knew of Lazarus' condition until he was raised from the dead. Jesus loved Lazarus. He surely wanted, in his humanity, to get to Lazarus as soon as possible to see him raised. Yet, the Father apparently had a significant delay in mind. Only when the Father was prepared to raise Lazarus from the dead was the Spirit of the Lord present for raising Lazarus. Jesus knew from the beginning that the end result would not be death. Rather, the Father was acting in the circumstances for His glory so that Jesus could be glorified through raising Lazarus to life. (John 11:4) Until the Father was raising Lazarus, Jesus had no power to do so.

So What Are We to Do?

Experience has taught Nancy and me to inquire what the Father is doing before we begin praying for anyone. That inquiry is made on several fronts.

Ask the person. Let the person seeking healing explain what is desired or what the problem is. Do not cut the request short. If the person is not sure how to start, you can say, "tell me where it hurts." Many times, the person requesting prayer will offer insights into the nature and source of the problem. Gentle, probing questions often illuminate a fuller picture of what is needed. Don't be in a hurry to start praying. The person's answers do not necessarily tell us what the Father is doing but rather the person's understanding of the need. The answers seldom tell us *all* the Father is doing.

Listen to the person. Listen to the answer of where it hurts and give plenty of time to receive other complaints.

Listen to the Holy Spirit. While listening to the answer from the person, we have learned to also listen to the Holy Spirit. An unspoken question to the Holy Spirit about what is going on often provides insights into the source or true nature of the problem. A surprising number of physical ailments coincide with some spiritual difficulty or some hurtful experience. We believe that praying for the sick, injured or tormented is simply not complete without inquiring of the Holy Spirit what else is going on.

Listen while praying. While the prayer continues, keep seeking the mind of the Holy Spirit about what else is happening. It is not uncommon to start praying for one issue and end up praying for another apparently unrelated issue. Once the dam breaks all the water can come out. When the Holy Spirit and the person are apparently done describing the nature and source of the problem, we assume that we have heard all we will hear and have seen all we will see as to what the Father is doing – until we start praying. During the prayer, we continue to listen to the Spirit and to watch the person. We also pay attention to such things as heat in the body, trembling and other uncommon phenomena. Praying with a group of spirit filled Christians who understand and apply this approach often leads to words of knowledge and words of wisdom from one or more in the group. Let those words of knowledge and words of wisdom provide the direction for more prayer.

Don't be in a hurry to finish. Our prayers tend to be of short duration. We don't believe that God needs a consultant or advisor on what to do to heal the person. We are partial to the eight words Moses used in praying for Miriam to be healed of leprosy. *"Heal her now, Oh God, I beseech thee."* (Numbers 12:13) Miraculous healing often continues well after the active prayer is concluded. We often get done before God does. Through time we have been able to sense, on occasion, that God is still acting. In those circumstances, we do not hesitate to tell the person being prayed for to wait expectantly because God is not done yet.

Check for manifestation of the presence of God. While praying for the things revealed to you by the person and the Holy Spirit, be on the alert for the *manifestation of the presence* of God. Each of us probably experiences the manifestation of God's presence differently. For me, His presence manifests as a full body goose bump. Nancy gets oil on her hands or shiny gold particles we refer to as "gold dust." Others report they simply know that He is present by the peace that settles on them and the situation. However God's presence is manifested for you, when you feel/sense it, take that as encouragement that you are on the right track and that God is not done yet. It is not the least uncommon for the presence of God to continue manifesting for a period of time following the exhaustion of the words God has given. Do not be afraid of silence. Once you have begun praying, and the Spirit of the Lord is present to heal, stay out of the way. Enjoy yourself as you soak in His presence but understand that continuing to babble does not increase the power of God. Most of the time, we are done praying before God is done healing.

Check for results. When you perceive that God is done acting, ask the person to check for results. If he couldn't move his ankle, ask him to move his ankle. If the condition is improved but not perfect, do not hesitate to pray again. When Jesus restored sight to one man He asked how the man could see. *"I see men as trees, walking,"* he reported. (Mark 8:22-25) Jesus prayed again and his sight was fully restored. Do not be afraid to repeat or continue your prayers if you encounter a "trees walking" experience.

Beware of "canned" prayers. If you know in advance the words you will use, be cautious. Many who have prayed fervently for years for issues such as back pain may develop a formula "back prayer" irrespective of whether or not that prayer has been effective in the past. The person requesting prayer will receive the formula "back prayer" and assume that is the end of the issue.

Beginning the prayer immediately seems to interfere with my ability to hear from God about the nature and extent of the problem. I sometimes simply wait until the "formula prayers" are concluded and then start a gentle inquiry. Occasionally, a word of knowledge or wisdom will come during the "formula prayers" but the formula prayers are so distracting that I find it more difficult to hear.

Remember that Jesus the man did not become able to heal following His Baptism with the Holy Spirit. Neither do we. We still are completely dependent upon God for healing, whether instantly or over time. It simply isn't us. Since Jesus couldn't do it, I am confident I cannot do it. Miraculous healing starts and ends with God. This knowledge reinforces the need to see and hear what the Father is doing.

In a real sense, our prayers become prophetic utterances of what the Father is doing. If we are praying for what the Father is doing, then the declaration carries with it the backing of heaven. Just like all prophecy, however, the speaker is simply a mouthpiece, announcing realities that are wholly dependent upon the power of another and delivered under the authority granted by that other. Even though we speak the testimony of Jesus which is the Spirit of prophecy, the power begins and ends with God, not us.

What About Qualifications?

I cannot comprehend a promise that I can do what God alone can do, much less greater things than those. But, I can handle a promise that I can do what a man in right relation to God the Father did, and greater things that these. All I need is access to the same power and authorization to use it.

The authorization to access God's power as Jesus did is to have the same standing before the Father as Jesus had. The good news is that we have that very standing. Because of what Jesus did, we are the righteousness of God in Christ.

> *Therefore, if anyone is in Christ, he is a new creation; the old has gone, the new has come! All this is from God, who reconciled us to himself through Christ and gave us the ministry of reconciliation: that God was reconciling the world to himself in Christ, not counting men's sins against them. And he has committed to us the message of reconciliation.*

We are therefore Christ's ambassadors, as though God were making his appeal through us. We implore you on Christ's behalf: Be reconciled to God. God made him who had no sin to be sin for us, so that in him we might become the righteousness of God. (2 Corinthians 5:17-21)

Jesus was in good standing before God because He committed no sin. God has reconciled us to Him through Jesus and is no longer counting our sins against us. Jesus is the righteousness of God. Since God put all our sin on Jesus, we can become the righteousness of God through faith in Jesus. We stand before God the Father in the same earthly shoes that Jesus wore.

From where does this righteousness of God come? Faith in Jesus. From where does our salvation come? Faith in Jesus. What is the qualifying requirement to do those things Jesus had been doing? Faith in Jesus. Do I detect a pattern here?

CHAPTER TWELVE

No Disqualification By Prior Acts

Some refuse to participate in miracles, signs and wonders out of a sense of unworthiness. The source of this feeling is an awareness of past and current sin. This "sin-awareness" severely inhibits participation in things of God.

No Disqualification From Ministry

Think about the most prevalent ministries found in most churches. An awareness of current or past sin seldom inhibits believers from cooking for the church supper, cleaning up after functions, feeding the hungry, or caring for children during adult activities. If a ministry does not require God to "show up" then that ministry can be performed with equal results by any service organization.

Fewer people choose to participate in ministries when accomplishment of the ministry goal requires God to act. The attitude seems to be that if God is required, He won't show up if a sinner is present. This is totally the opposite of what Jesus said. Jesus "hung out" with sinners. He came to save sinners, not the "righteous." (Matthew 9:12-13; Mark 2:16-17; Luke 5:30-32)

This sin awareness is facilitated and enhanced by an accuser. The more an accuser points out the presence of current sin or brings to mind past sin, the greater the awareness. It is not coincidental that the name *satan* means "accuser." One of his main ploys is to point out our inability to conform our conduct to the law, thereby creating humiliation and shame.

The good news is that the accuser has been cast down. Michael and the angels fought with the accuser who was found to be too weak. He lost his place in heaven and was hurled down to earth.

> *"Now have come the salvation and the power and the kingdom of our God, and the authority of his Christ. For the accuser of our brothers, who accuses them before our God day and night, has been hurled down. They overcame him by the blood of the Lamb and by the word of their testimony; they did not love their lives so much as to shrink from death."* (Revelation 12:10-11)

The devil has no truth in him. *"When he lies, he speaks his native language, for he is a liar and the father of lies."* (John 8:44) The truth sets us free. (John 8:32) If the truth set us free, lies imprison us. The only way a lie can imprison someone is if the lie is believed. By believing a lie, the liar is empowered.

The Apostle Paul is an excellent example of the truth that past bad actions do not disqualify a believer from ministry in the present and in the future. Paul breathed *"out murderous threats against the Lord's disciples. He went to the high priest and asked him for letters to the synagogues in Damascus, so that if he found any there who belonged to the Way, whether men or women, he might take them as prisoners to Jerusalem."* (Acts 9:1-2) Paul was "a blasphemer and a persecutor and a violent man." (1 Timothy 1:13) He stood by in approval at the stoning of Stephen. (Acts 8:1) He described himself as the chief sinner. (1 Timothy 1:15)

Paul experienced a prolonged period of unbelief. No matter how long the past period of unbelief, the only relevant time period in the kingdom is now. The very second you become a believer the years, even eons, of unbelief disappear in the twinkling of an eye. It doesn't matter how long you may have believed that God was no longer in the healing business. It doesn't matter how long you may have believed that miracles, signs and wonders passed away with the canonization of the New Testament or the passing of the apostolic age. As soon as those beliefs (unbeliefs?) are set aside, the past record of unbelief no longer matters.

Now compared to Paul's history, what have you done that is so bad? You are just as forgiven as Paul. Your past is simply irrelevant to your present and your future ministry opportunities. It is impossible for you to have been worse than Paul in the context of unbelief. He not only did not believe in Jesus as the Messiah, he wanted to kill any who did believe. How can you think you surpass him?

Paul didn't do so well following his conversion either. He was unable to conform his conduct to the requirements of the law.

> *"I do not understand what I do. For what I want to do I do not do, but what I hate I do. And if I do what I do not want to do, I agree that the law is good. As it is, it is no longer I myself who do it, but it is sin living in me. I know that nothing good lives in me, that is, in my sinful nature. For I have the desire to do what is good, but I cannot carry it out. For what I do is not the good I want to do; no, the evil I do not want to do – this I keep on doing."* (Romans 7:15-19)

Paul was thoroughly disgusted with himself. "What a wretched man I am! Who will rescue me from this body of death?" (Romans 7:24) The devil wants us to forget that we are in the same boat with Paul. He wants us to not be fellow workers with God, as Paul was. If the devil can keep us out of the game, others will be impacted.

Every church board, every great and mighty ministry existing since the death and resurrection of Jesus Christ is populated one hundred percent with people who keep on doing evil, just like Paul. It is pride in our sin that makes us feel that we are worse than Paul, not worthy to co-labor with God. What can be worse conduct than to keep on doing the evil that you do not want to do? Yet, that is exactly what Paul did.

False humility causes believers to exalt their bad behavior as a disqualifying factor. Their sin awareness makes them want to crucify themselves. To those believers, I say, "Get off the cross, we need the wood." Since *"there is now no condemnation for those who are in Christ Jesus"* (Romans 8:1), get over it and get busy.

Choose Who You Will Believe

There are two competing voices, Jesus and the liar. Choose which one you will believe. Will you continue to believe that you are a miserable sinner with no redeeming qualities in you and completely worthless to God in ministry? Or, will you believe that your relationship to God qualifies you for a life of miracles, signs and wonders?

God has been offering a choice since the time of Moses.

> *"See, I set before you today life and prosperity, death and destruction. . . . This day I call heaven and earth as witnesses against you that I have set before you life and death, blessings and curses. Now choose life, so that you and your children may live and that you may love the LORD your God, listen to his voice, and hold fast to him."* (Deuteronomy 30:15-20)

In order to believe you are disqualified, you must call God a liar. The Word declares:

- God made him who had no sin to be sin for us, so that in him we might become the righteousness of God. (2 Cor. 5:21);
- If anyone is in Christ, he is a new creation; the old has gone, the new has come; (2 Cor. 5:17)
- Sin shall not be your master, because you are not under law, but under grace. You have been set free from sin and have become slaves to righteousness; (Romans 6:14-18)
- God reconciled the world to Himself in Christ, not counting men's sins against them; (2 Cor. 5:19) and
- God forgives my wickedness and will remember my sins no more. (Hebrews 8:12)

In regard to ministry, the Word is clear:

- The blood of Christ cleansed our consciences from acts that lead to death so that we may serve the living God; (Hebrews 9:14) and
- We are God's workmanship, created in Christ Jesus to do good works, which God prepared in advance for us to do; (Ephesians 2:10)

Our service to God is made possible by the cleansing of Jesus' blood. He cleaned us up for ministry. When we become alive in Jesus, we are a new creation which is designed to do good works. The good works are not the things we imagine. Rather, they are the good works that God has prepared in advance for us to do. God has prepared good works for us to perform while we are yoked together with Jesus, whose yoke is easy and whose burden is light. (Matthew 11:30)

"By one sacrifice Jesus has made perfect forever those who are being made holy." (Hebrews 10:14) While the process of sanctification continues in

your life, your status before God is that you have been made perfect forever. I am qualified to participate in miracles, signs and wonders due to the status conferred on me by what Jesus did. The status He has conferred upon me cannot be ruined by my shortcomings.

The woman who wiped Jesus' feet with her tears and poured perfume on Him while He visited the Pharisee's house was a notorious sinner. However, she left that night smelling just like Jesus. (Luke 7:36-39)

No Disqualification From Being Healed

God heals His people because He is good, not because His people are good. He heals as a manifestation of His love, not as a reward for good behavior. He heals because He is worthy of glory, honor and praise, not because His people are worthy.

The sin awareness problem also prevents many from seeking healing or delivery from torment. Just as in the ministry context, the attitude seems to be that God would not choose to heal me or deliver me from torment because of my attitudes or actions, either in the present or in the past.

The prior section of this chapter is equally applicable to the person who seeks healing or delivery from torment as it is applicable to those who would be praying for that person. Whether involved in ministry or seeking the compassion of God, the born again believer's status is the same.

Some men came to Jesus to seek healing for a paralytic. They lowered the paralytic through the roof on his mat. Jesus saw the faith of those bringing the paralytic and said to the paralytic, *"Friend, your sins are forgiven."* After some discussion with the Pharisees and teachers of the law, Jesus demonstrated his authority to announce forgiveness of sin by commanding the paralytic to *"get up, take your mat and go home."* (Luke 4:18-24)

Jesus did not:

- command the paralytic to repent;
- question whether the paralytic wanted a saving relationship with the Son of God;
- send the paralytic off to fast and pray for a period of time to become worthy of healing;
- condition the paralytic's healing on a particular attitude or thought pattern;
- seek a promise of changed behavior; or

- require a sacrifice at the temple.

Rather, Jesus simply announced that the paralytic's sins were forgiven.

Jesus knew that *"the power of the Lord was present for him to heal the sick."* (Luke 5:17) He knew from His prayers with the Father that the Father was healing His people who asked. He knew that God was delivering His compassion to His people irrespective of their compliance or non-compliance with the sacrificial system in place for the forgiveness of sins. In short, Jesus knew the Father had not withheld His power to heal the sick in any instance recorded in the scriptures based upon a sin-condition.

Jesus healed *all* the people who came to Him seeking healing. He delivered *all* the people from torment who came to Him seeking deliverance. Jesus *"is the radiance of God's glory and the exact representation of His being, sustaining all things by His powerful word."* (Hebrews 1:3) Jesus was representing the Father *exactly* whenever He healed anyone or delivered anyone from torment. Since Jesus never conditioned healing or deliverance on proper standing in the sacrificial system, we know that the Father imposed no such limitation on the delivery of His compassion to His people.

CHAPTER THIRTEEN

No Excuses

When Nancy and I taught our first class on miracles, signs and wonders, the participants came from many different denominational backgrounds. In one of the first sessions, we asked about the "rules" for healing which the class members had been taught through the years. In short order, we had a list of twenty-five "rules" which people genuinely believed concerning miracles, signs and wonders. Most of those rules attempted to tie actions and attitudes, either on the part of the person praying or on the part of the person requesting prayer, to God's willingness to miraculously heal.

Nancy and I had experienced numerous miraculous healings through the years. Others in the class had also either been healed or seen a miraculous healing. Over a period of a couple weeks, the class examined these prior miraculous healings to determine if any of the rules applied to any of the healings.

Examination of those prior experiences completely debunked each of the "rules." In each instance, the prior reported miraculous healing violated one or more of the rules (and quite often all of them). In each instance, no rule could be identified that would explain the occurrence of the miraculous healing. It quickly became apparent the "rules" for healing were not rules after all. The "rules" seemed to have been born out of an attempt to explain the apparent lack of manifestation of a miraculous healing. The "rules" clearly had no causative effect. Rather, they were excuses for no results.

Study of the Word reveals two simple rules for divine healing and delivery from torment.

- We can do nothing by ourselves.
- Jesus is the healer.

The writings of many who lived in the late 1800's and early 1900's and experienced massive displays of miracles, signs and wonders reveal a common thread. All believed and understood that the miracle worker is always Jesus. Miracles are not worked by men in their own power having received a special gift. It is always Him.

A. B. Simpson (1843-1919), the founder of the Christian and Missionary Alliance, wrote clearly on the subject.

> "I wish to speak to you about Jesus, and Jesus only. I often hear people say, "I wish I could get hold of Divine Healing, but I cannot." Sometimes they say, "I have got it." If I ask them, "What have you got?" the answer is sometimes, "I have got the blessing", sometimes it is, "I have got the theory"; sometimes it is, "I have got the healing"; sometimes, "I have got the sanctification." But I thank God we have been taught that it is not the blessing, it is not the healing, it is not the sanctification, it is not the thing, it is not the it that you want, but it is something better. It is "the Christ"; it is Himself. (A. B. Simpson, *Himself*)

John Alexander Dowie (1847-1907) the founder of the Divine Healing Association of Australia and New Zealand, founder of the Christian Catholic Apostolic Church and Divine Healing Mission, and the founder of Zion, Illinois, also wrote on this subject.

> "Let it be supposed that the following words are a conversation between the reader [A] and the writer [B].
>
> A: What does this question mean? Do you really suppose that God has some one especial way of healing in these days of which men may know and avail themselves?
>
> B: That is exactly my meaning, and I wish very much that you should know God's Way of Healing, as I have done for many years.

A: What is the way, in your opinion?

B: You should rather ask, WHO is God's way? For the Way is a Person, not a thing. I will answer your question in His own words, "I am the Way, and the Truth, and the Life; no one cometh unto the Father, but by Me." These words were spoken by our Lord Jesus Christ, the Eternal Son of God, who is both Savior and our Healer. (John 14:6)" (Dowie, *Do You Know God's Way of Healing?*)

John G. Lake (1870-1935), who was greatly influenced by the healing ministry of John Alexander Dowie and ran "Healing Rooms," a healing center in Spokane, Washington, with over 100,000 documented healings in just five years, also wrote on this subject.

"God's way of healing is a person, not a thing. Jesus said. "I am the way, the truth, and the life." And He has ever been revealed to His people in all the ages by the Covenant Name, Jehovah Rophi, or, "I am the Lord that healeth thee," (John 14:6 and Exodus 15:26)

The Lord Jesus Christ is still the healer. He cannot change, for "*He is the same yesterday, today, and forever,*" and He is still with us, for He said, "*Lo, I am with you always, even unto the end of the world.*" (Hebrews 13:8 and Matthew 28:20.) Because He is unchangeable, and because He is present, in Spirit, just as when in the flesh. He is the healer of His people." (Lake, *God's Way of Healing*)

Jesus is not a puppet controlled by man. His awesome power is not dependent upon either the person praying or the person receiving prayer. Divine healing is a product solely dependent upon His nature and goodness.

There are no reports of Jesus refusing to perform a miraculous healing. It is not in the book. Peter explained to the centurion, Cornelius, and his household:

"*God anointed Jesus of Nazareth with the Holy Ghost and with power: who went about doing good, and healing all that were oppressed of the devil; for God was with him.*" (Acts 10:38 KJV)

Jesus did not heal *some* that were oppressed of the devil. He healed *all* who were oppressed of the devil. Scripture recounts many instances in which Jesus healed them *all*. (Matthew 4:24; 8:16; 9:35; 12:15; 14:36; Mark 6:56; Luke 4:40; 6:19)

Formulate Your Theology on What God Is Doing

The recounting of the testimony of Jesus, as prophecy, changes the atmosphere such that God's desires and purposes will be fulfilled. In other words, it is more likely that Jesus will do again what He has done in the past when the testimony of Jesus is given. It does not matter if the testimony is what Jesus did while He walked the earth or just last week. Jesus is still doing all that He did before.

"*The testimony of Jesus is the spirit of prophecy.*" (Revelation 19:10) Prophecy is God's word announced through human vessels. If God is not speaking, it is not prophecy. God's word does not return to Him empty, accomplishes what He desires and achieves the purpose for which He sent it. (Isaiah 55:11) The testimony of Jesus is the truth of what He has done or is doing.

The testimony of Jesus does not include what *apparently* did *not* happen. Guesses and surmises of what was *not perceived* serve no purpose. There is no prophecy involved there. The atmosphere will not be changed by a recitation of what was not observed. The creative power of the Word of God is not involved with reports of what apparently did not happen.

Beware of Theology Based on What God Did Not Do

Be particularly cautious when "interpreting" God's Word to discern rules or biblical principles concerning miraculous healing. It is dangerous to think that we can turn over a coin and properly interpret the other side. It is much safer to take Jesus at His word rather than try to figure out what Jesus would have announced in a different circumstance. In this context, it is dangerous to construct a theology to attempt to explain why a healing was not manifested in a particular instance. We have no scripture precedent for such rules.

Scripture is clear about not adding to what is recorded.

> "*Every word of God is flawless; . . . Do not add to His words, or He will rebuke you and prove you a liar.*" (Proverbs 30:5-6)

"If anyone adds anything to them, God will add to him the plagues described in this book. And if anyone takes words away from this book of prophecy, God will take away from him his share in the tree of life and in the holy city, which are described in this book." (Revelation 22:18-19)

Limitations on Our Observations

We do not have the ability to completely comprehend what Jesus is doing and when He is doing it. An *apparent* lack of a miraculous healing tells us nothing.

An example of the limitations of our powers of observation is the wedding feast in Cana. When Jesus turned the water into wine, no one knew *when* the miracle occurred. There was a manifestation at the pouring of the wine that the water had been transformed. But, who knew? The master of the banquet did not know that the wine had ever been water.

Scripture does not disclose who knew of the miracle, when it occurred, or even whether one had been attempted! No one had the complete picture but God Himself.

The occurrence of the miracle did not necessarily coincide with the perception of the miracle. Indeed, the perception was not necessarily that there had been a miracle at all until the servants reported that they had drawn off water for purification, delivered it to the master of the banquet, and that the master had complimented the bridegroom on the best wine. (John 2:1-10)

It is best to take Jesus at His word and not attempt to fill in the blanks from our own intellect.

CHAPTER FOURTEEN

No Experts Required

I t doesn't take an expert to participate in miracles, signs and wonders. God has not limited His activities in divine healing, for example, to a select few who have received an anointing specifically for healing. I am *not* saying there is not an anointing for healing. I *am* saying that every believer has the power and authority to pray for divine healing, for himself and others.

Nancy and I have experienced a significant boost in the number of miracles, signs and wonders we have seen. We claim no "healing anointing" or special ability whatsoever. Quite the opposite! We know beyond doubt that we are mere pawns on the chessboard of divine healing and delivery from torment. Just as in chess, all men have only one function, to serve the King.

Nancy has become bolder in praying out loud. She felt for many years that she just didn't have the flowery speech and "gift of gab" in her communication with God that she thought she heard in the audible prayers of others. Consequently, although she prayed fervently, she seldom prayed out loud and was almost never the leader in audible prayer.

About three weeks into our pursuit of miracles, signs and wonders, we visited a Thursday night ministry in Ruidoso where I have been permitted to deliver God's message on many occasions. Nancy had been praying for a renewal of God's compassion in her. There was a time when she just wasn't as moved by the suffering of others as she felt she should be. She was finding God's compassion returning to her. While at the Thursday night meeting, she was asked to share about the healing of her hands. When she was done sharing, I launched into one of my favorite messages.

In the middle of the message, one of the men in attendance got a phone call – don't you just love cell phones? He had recently had surgery for brain cancer and feared the remission his doctors were reporting was a false report. I had spoken with him before the meal, introducing myself because I was certain from his appearance that we had never met. When he told me his name, I realized this man was someone we had known for a few years. His appearance was so different I had not recognized him. He apologized for needing to leave and started for the door. I had promised him that we would pray for him before the night was over so I stopped my message and we started praying for him. Many joined in the laying on of hands while we prayed for salvation assurance, physical healing and delivery from torment.

When we concluded our prayers, he turned to Nancy and said, "I want *her* to pray for me. My hands and my feet hurt me so much."

Nancy was moved to tears as she asked God to heal his hands and feet and to deliver the shalom of heaven upon this man. He then left and I returned to my message.

In bed in the middle of the night, Nancy lay awake worrying whether she had let this man down due to the "inadequacy" of her prayer. Had she asked confidently enough? Had she demonstrated enough faith? Were the words sufficient? Had the compassion she felt which moved her to tears been delivered? Would Frank die because she did something "wrong."

We have known for centuries that it doesn't take an expert to pray with someone for salvation. We don't seek someone with a "special anointing" to lead another in the sinner's prayer for redemption. Yet we have developed an idea that it takes an expert to pray for healing and delivery from torment.

That Thursday night God told Nancy unmistakably that it doesn't take an expert to pray for healing and delivery from torment. God spoke in a nearly audible voice to Nancy, telling her that it didn't matter how she prayed. It didn't matter what words she used. It didn't matter if she understood the source of the physical symptoms of pain and suffering. God said, in essence, "I am the healer. It is not up to you. Just ask."

This message brought Nancy great relief and confidence. She no longer worries that her prayers may not sound "professional enough." She is convinced that asking in confidence is the key. The healing is never done by the asker; it is always done by God. She has decided to relax and ask, remembering how insignificant we are in delivering the power to heal.

Although we are insignificant, we are commissioned to ask the One who has the power.

After the Ruidoso trip, God spoke to Nancy shortly after we had turned out the lights on a Saturday night. She "heard" God clearly telling her that He would be in our home the next night and would be healing people. All I knew was that while I was holding her in our bed she started sobbing. She sat up in bed and haltingly asked me, "What would you say if I told you that God just told me He would be here tomorrow night and would be healing people?"

I responded, "I would say we need to announce that at church in the morning and then open our house."

The next morning we approached our pastor about making the announcement. He informed us that his sermon was going to be on healing. He anticipated a prayer time for healing at the end of the service. He was happy to permit us to announce what God had told Nancy.

We were permitted to give our testimonies about the recent healing of Nancy's hands and my back. After the service, several people stood at the front of the church and prayed for those asking for healing. As we prayed, God repeatedly healed people with problems in their hands, backs, knees and feet. The percentage of those healed in our prayer line was so high I wondered if there would be anyone left for healing at our house that evening.

That night twenty four people arrived at our house. I gave a short explanation of why we were there and what we understood God was up to at this time. Then, we just asked. Nearly everyone there both received prayer and prayed for the others. There were no experts so far as we could tell. We were just people gathered in assurance that God is still in the healing business and business is good.

We witnessed significant healings that night. The praying went on for about four hours. During some of that time, Nancy and I were involved in the laying on of hands. At other times, we were across the room simply agreeing with others who were taking the "laboring oar." I could detect no difference in the reliability of God's response depending on who was praying. He was simply and profoundly pouring out His compassion on His people

Since then we more often seek out opportunities to pray for people, both at church services and "as we go." We have found that God's Superstore for Healing and Delivery from Torment knows no geographical limitations.

It is not a "big box" store. No four walls can contain it. Rather, it is a movable feast.

Nancy and I were very "impressed" when we went to Sojourn Church in Carrolton, Texas, to hear Bill Johnson that neither he nor his team which accompanied him did the praying. The praying for healing was done by the un-schooled, uneducated, believers assembled there, praying for strangers in most instances, in prayers lasting less than two minutes. The "experts" were watching and enjoying as God manifested His presence, His power and healing that night.

No series of classes will equip anyone to perform divine healing. It is not the person praying who heals. It is Jesus Himself who heals. That explanation is at the same time simple and profound beyond our ability to understand. We cannot learn the mechanism. We will not learn any magic incantations. We will not discover any secrets that will put God in a box.

We can be absolutely certain that God's objectives and goals remain the same. We can have no such assurance that we understand how He will manifest His power in any particular circumstance to bring His objectives and goals to reality. He doesn't work the same way every time. He doesn't want us to think that He is a puppet and we are the puppet masters. We miss the boat when we expect that God will always act in the same manner.

When we realize it is God who does the healing, we are not as likely to search for someone with a "greater anointing" when presented with a sizable problem. I can't heal a sprained ankle. I also can't heal cancer. Only God can heal anyone of anything. The good news is He is just as *able* to heal cancer as He is to heal the sprained ankle. He is just as *willing* to heal cancer as He is to heal the sprained ankle. Just ask. Only believe.

What are you waiting for? What are you afraid of? Trust me, you are not big enough to get in God's way when He is pouring out His compassion on His people. If you ask wrong, you need not worry so long as you are asking the One with the power to heal. He doesn't need a consultant. He doesn't need an assistant. He's not wondering what is wrong in the situation. He is not going to withhold His blessing if you command vertebrae to line up if the problem is not with the vertebrae but rather in the muscle. Quit being so concerned with your reputation. No one truly expects that *you* will heal them.

You and I need only believe. From that belief will come a greater willingness to ask.

CHAPTER FIFTEEN

The Great Commission

I am familiar with the "Great Commission" primarily because I have been afraid it might apply to me, requiring me to leave my comfort zone and go into the world. There are several versions of the Great Commission. The most familiar passage is found in the Gospel of Matthew.

> *"Then Jesus came to them and said, 'All authority in heaven and on earth has been given to me. Therefore go and make disciples of all nations, baptizing them in the name of the Father and of the Son and of the Holy Spirit, and teaching them to obey everything I have commanded you. And surely I am with you always, to the very end of the age.'"* (Matthew 28:18-20)

The Greek word translated "go" in verse 19 is *poreuomai*. Another meaning for *poreuomai* is "to pursue the journey on which one has entered, to continue on one's journey." Jesus' command did not concern the *going* so much as it concerned *what to do while going*.

Another way of expressing the same thing would be "as you go," make disciples. This alternate translation is a two edged sword. While I apparently am not commanded to go anywhere new, I am charged with the duty to make disciples *as I go*.

Making disciples is an all day, every day, job given to all believers. Or, was the Great Commission limited to just the Apostles? I am either included in the Great Commission or I am not. Jesus either intended to limit this Commission to the Apostles or it is a commission to all believers.

If the commission is limited to the Apostles, who is it that is going to make disciples of those who never met the Apostles?

The best news in the Great Commission is Jesus' assurance that He is "with you always, to the very end of the age." We may have a big job – to make disciples of all nations – but we are not alone.

Let's talk about the word "commission." Jesus did not use that word. Rather, his directive has been *described* as the Great Commission. "Commission," as a noun, primarily refers to an instruction, command, or duty. A commission includes with it the authority to perform the assigned task. One who receives a commission to act also receives all authority necessary to do that act. The one giving a commission must have the authority both to do the thing commissioned and to authorize another to do it *in his stead*.

Did Jesus have that type of authority? He precedes the commission with the statement, *"All authority in heaven and on earth has been given to me."* The Greek word translated "authority" is *exousia* which means delegated influence, authority, jurisdiction, liberty, power, right and strength. Jesus was given all *exousia*, both in heaven and on earth. He not only has *some exousia*, He has *all exousia*. Jesus not only had the authority to make disciples, He had the authority to delegate his authority, to authorize *someone else* to act whenever and however He deemed necessary.

The real question is not *whether* Jesus could delegate the authority. The only question is, *to whom*? The Great Commission commands a continuation of Jesus' work. It involves doing what He did. He promised that *anyone who has faith in* Him will do what He did – and even greater things than those. (John 14:12) Jesus made disciples. Therefore, anyone who has faith in Him will make disciples. How could the Great Commission, then, be limited to the Apostles? *"Anyone who has faith in Him"* is not limited to the Apostles. Jesus meant what He said. It is the *"anyones"* who will do what He did.

The Gospel of Mark records Jesus instructing the Eleven:

> *"Later Jesus appeared to the Eleven. . . . He said to them, 'Go into all the world and preach the good news to all creation. Whoever believes and is baptized will be saved, but whoever does not believe will be condemned. And these signs will accompany those who believe: In my name they will drive out demons; they will speak in new tongues; they will pick up snakes with their hands; and when they drink deadly*

poison, it will not hurt them at all; they will place their hands on sick people, and they will get well.' After the Lord Jesus had spoken to them, he was taken up into heaven and he sat at the right hand of God. Then the disciples went out and preached everywhere, and the Lord worked with them and confirmed his word by the signs that accompanied it."
(Mark 16:14-20)

Jesus said *"these signs will accompany those who believe."* Jesus did not say "these signs will accompany you eleven." Rather, the signs accompany those who believe – the very same *anyones* who will do what Jesus had been doing.

Jesus promised that those who believe *"will place their hands on sick people and they will get well."* We are instructed to place our hands on the sick. God will do the rest. Jesus promised the sign of healing sick people to those who believe. The disciples went out and preached. Jesus worked with them, through the Holy Spirit, to confirm His word by the accompanying signs. However, Jesus did not promise to confirm His word by accompanying signs only for the Apostles. He made that promise to all of us *anyones*.

James also promises that the Lord will raise up the sick.

"Is any one of you sick? He should call the elders of the church to pray over him and anoint him with oil in the name of the Lord. And the prayer offered in faith will make the sick person well; the Lord will raise him up. If he has sinned, he will be forgiven. Therefore confess your sins to each other and pray for each other so that you may be healed. The prayer of a righteous man is powerful and effective." (James 5:14-16)

James' command to call the elders of the church signals clearly that the great commission is not limited to the Apostles only. There is no magic to the difference of laying on hands as promised by Jesus and anointing with oil as commanded by James. In both instances, the healer is Jesus, not the hands or the oil. The point is that the promise is made to all of us *anyones*.

John records a short version of the Great Commission:

"As the Father has sent me, I am sending you.' (John 20:21)

Jesus sends us *as He was sent*. We have access to the same authority and same power of God which was available to Jesus. The very same Holy Spirit who empowered Jesus lives in us. We did not receive Holy Spirit, Jr. or Holy Spirit, Lite (upgrade available through payment of an additional fee).

The Father sent Jesus

- anointed with the Holy Spirit and with power; and
- He went around doing good, healing all who were oppressed by the devil,
- because God was with Him. (Acts 10:38)

Therefore, Jesus sends us,

- anointed with the Holy Spirit and with power; and
- we are to go around doing good, healing all who were oppressed by the devil,
- because God is with us.

When, you ask, was this anointing with the Holy Spirit and with power? Jesus foretold the Baptism with the Holy Spirit and said,

> *"I am going to send you what my Father has promised; but stay in the city until you have been clothed with power from on high."* (Luke 24:49)

If we are to be "clothed with power" we are going to put something external all around us to both protect us and to be what others see when they observe us. Jesus was promising new clothes, power from on high.

Then Jesus continued,

> *"Do not leave Jerusalem, but wait for the gift my Father promised, which you have heard me speak about. For John baptized with water, but in a few days you will be baptized with the Holy Spirit. But you will receive power when the Holy Spirit comes on you; and you will be my witnesses in Jerusalem, and in all Judea and Samaria, and to the ends of the earth."* (Acts 1:4-8)

"What my Father has promised" is baptism with the Holy Spirit. Jesus is very clear that the power is *"from on high"* and the power is received *"when the Holy Spirit comes on you."*

The promised power equips the recipient to be Jesus' witness "to the ends of the earth." The primary function of a witness is to report the acts of Jesus, that is *the testimony of Jesus*" which Revelation tells us is *the spirit of prophecy*." (Revelation 19:10)

Our experience has shown that giving the testimony of Jesus prior to praying for healing seems to enhance the likelihood of miraculous healing. Before praying for healing, we make a determined effort to give the testimony of Jesus, either the historical record from the scriptures or the recent history of miraculous interventions we have witnessed.

Baptism with the Holy Spirit was not restricted to the Apostles. John reports that Jesus will baptize "you" with the Holy Spirit. John described the group he was addressing as a brood of vipers, a group including both Pharisees and Sadducees. It was to these people John announced that Jesus "will baptize you with the Holy Spirt and with fire." (Matthew 3:7-11; Luke 3:7-16; John 1:24-34)

The Pharisees enjoyed such favor with Jesus that He called them "whitewashed tombs," "full of dead men's bones and everything unclean," and "full of hypocrisy and wickedness." (Matthew 23:27-28) Yet, it was to these people that John announced that Jesus would baptize *them* with the Holy Spirit and with fire. Not the apostles, the Pharisees. The promised baptism with the Holy Spirit is a promise to all believers, not the Apostles alone.

The various forms of the Great Commission make it clear that Jesus sent all believers, just as the Father had sent Him, to "make disciples," and to "preach the good news to all creation" while God is confirming His word by the signs that accompany it.

CHAPTER SIXTEEN
Hosting His Presence

The Presence of God can be sensed. God manifests His Presence in different ways to different people. It is sometimes difficult to recognize what your particular manifestation may be since God may have been manifesting Himself in the same way to you for a long time without any impact on you.

When I sense His Presence, I feel like I am electric, like I have been plugged in to an electric outlet. My body reacts with a "whole body goose bump." When I first began feeling this sensation, I thought I was just reacting to the cold temperature of the room. When I began to suspect there was more to this reaction, I started paying attention to when it would occur. I soon realized it had nothing to do with too much air conditioning.

The first connection I noticed between the Presence of God and the circumstances was that His Presence would manifest while someone was giving the testimony of Jesus. If the conversation was focused on giving glory to God for what He had done, the Presence would manifest. I soon learned that as I was feeling my "whole body goose bump," Nancy would be experiencing the manifestation of God's Presence in the particular way she experiences it.

For a prolonged period of time, the phrase "the testimony of Jesus is the spirit of prophecy" would bring on the manifestation for both of us. Although I don't claim to understand that phrase yet, as the revelation of the meaning of that phrase has begun, the less the manifestation comes simply from saying the phrase.

Nancy and I are convinced there is a release of power from reciting the testimony of Jesus. For that reason, we are careful to give the testimony of Jesus before praying for healing. The closer the testimony is to the current problem, the more likely the manifestation will occur. The more the manifestation occurs, the more likely a miraculous healing is in store.

Jesus certainly sensed the Presence of the Holy Spirit as he went around doing good, healing all who were oppressed by the devil. Peter's full report of Jesus' actions is instructive.

> *"God anointed Jesus of Nazareth with the Holy Ghost and with power: who went about doing good, and healing all that were oppressed of the devil; for God was with him."* (Acts 10:38)

Jesus was able to heal all that were oppressed of the devil for only one reason. God was with Him. If God wasn't there, He couldn't do it.

Luke apparently sensed God's Presence also. He reports that "the power of the Lord was present for him to heal the sick." (Luke 5:17) Once the power was there, Jesus could announce forgiveness of sins and healing of the body.

The power of God cannot be separated from the Presence of God. He does not send His power unattended. And, He doesn't leave home without it. If the Presence of God is manifested in a place, the power of God is being manifested there to accomplish His purposes. Since Jesus is the same, yesterday, today and forever, those things Jesus is accomplishing through the power of God on Monday, He is accomplishing on the rest of the days of the week.

We have "learned" to be confident when the Presence of God is manifested. Nancy and I often feel that we are supposed to pray for someone as we go about our daily tasks, in the usual places. As we have done that more and more, a pattern has emerged. I would generally approach a person with a crutch, cane, hobble, cast or some such. I would inquire about the nature of the problem and what was currently happening. Most of the time, the Presence of God would be made manifest to Nancy and to me. When that happened, we would suggest that the Holy Spirit had His eyes on the person and would like to heal them. Then we ask for permission to pray for healing. We have been turned down only once – and we didn't sense the Presence of God on that occasion.

Our experience in these "drive by healings" has simply amazed us. Generally speaking, there is no time for long extended discussions of the theology of divine healing. There is, always, time for a recitation of the testimony of Jesus. We are confident that God is healing these people miraculously – even though we are not in church – even though there is not an organ in the corner playing soft music – even though a preacher has not just concluded an inspirational sermon. When God manifests His Presence we simply assume He wants to intervene miraculously in someone's history. Quite often, that assumption has been correct.

John the Baptist reported seeing the Spirit of God coming down as a dove *and remaining* on Jesus. He had been told that the one upon whom the Spirit came down *and remained* was the one who would baptize with the Holy Spirit. (John 1:32-22) The Presence of God remained on Jesus. That is, Jesus *hosted* the Presence of God. I can confidently report that Jesus performed absolutely no miracles without contemporaneously hosting the Presence.

Nancy and I have given up trying to clean up our acts. We simply are no good at it. However, we fervently desire to *host the Presence* of God. Our acts have been cleaned up simply by the desire to host the Presence. We know there are certain places, activities and attitudes that are not beneficial to us and in which God is not made welcome. We know better than to invite Him to accompany us there. We are afraid to "check the Presence at the door" and expect Him to be readily available when we leave those places or activities. Our actions have changed because we do not want to break the fellowship and not experience God's Presence.

Nancy is not a whole body goose bump person. Rather, the Presence of God manifests itself in her body by oil on her hands. Quite often there is gold, shiny stuff in that oil which can be rubbed on others or on her clothes or a napkin. When I feel the goose bumps, I turn to Nancy and say, "Check your hands." When we both have the manifestation, get ready to be prayed for, pretty much whether you like it or not.

Others with whom we meet regularly experience the Presence differently. Some just "sense" His Presence. Others feel a peace come into the circumstances. With practice, we have all gotten better at discerning when God is manifesting His Presence. It is a very exciting time.

We intentionally delay starting to pray for someone in an attempt to discern what the Father is doing. A sense of the Presence often seems to manifest in confirmation of a subject matter where the Father is acting. If we are praying concerning a particular matter and the Presence manifests, we take that as confirmation that the Father is healing that problem or dealing with that area of torment.

When the Presence does not manifest, we begin praying with the expectation that, as we get closer to the issue, the Presence will manifest. In most instances, the manifestation of God's presence occurs.

There are also times when there is no apparent manifestation of the Presence and a miraculous healing occurs nonetheless. God simply refuses to be placed in a box and to perform on cue. In those instances, we know that *"the eyes of the Lord are on the righteous and his ears are attentive to their prayer."* (1 Peter 3:12; Psalms 34:15) Neither His willingness to heal nor His power to accomplish His purposes is dependent upon our sensing His Presence. He is willing and able, whether or not we are sensing the Presence.

Finally, it is not uncommon for us to exhaust the words we know to pray in a situation while the Presence is still manifesting. In those instances, we have learned to wait upon the Lord while He continues to act in the situation. His power is completely unaffected by our silence. We try to encourage the affected person that God is still working and hasn't finished even though our prayers are done.

CHAPTER SEVENTEEN
Praying Out of Authority

Early in our adventure we encountered a test of our desire to participate in delivering God's compassion to His people. We had been praying for healing for awhile in church settings and in our home. We had not yet dared to approach a complete stranger in any other arena.

We like to eat breakfast at La Madeleine in Fort Worth. The drive to Fort Worth from Granbury gives us some time to get away from the press of legal work and the daily grind of life in Granbury. We also enjoy the food.

We had been going to La Madeleine often enough to start to recognize some faces but not often enough to have developed even a nodding acquaintance with anyone. One of the men I noticed was there nearly every time we went was an elderly man who walked with a cane and clearly was significantly impaired. The hitch in his git-a-long made it obvious he walked with a lot pain.

I found myself sitting where I would have to look directly at this man nearly each time we saw him. Either he would already be there and we would sit close by or he would come after we were located and sit close to us. He seemed to always sit alone and never seemed to be in a good mood. We called him the curmudgeon.

I began to sense that God was directing me to pray for this man. I would ask Nancy whether she believed we were supposed to pray for him. She was fairly certain she had not received any such direction. So, on several occasions we left the restaurant without approaching the curmudgeon, greatly relieved that we had not been inconvenienced or embarrassed by approaching him with an offer of prayer.

On each of those occasions, I would feel "hounded" by God all the way back to Granbury. I was embarrassed that I let my concerns for my reputation and my comfort override what was becoming a clear direction to pray for this man. Finally I told Nancy on the way back to Granbury, "The next time we see that guy at La Madeleine I am going to offer to pray for him. I am tired of fighting God all the way back to Granbury."

On our next trip to La Madeleine, there he was. This time he was not sitting alone but rather was at a table with three other folks we had never seen before. I ate a leisurely breakfast hoping he might leave before I had to act. He apparently was not in any hurry either. I looked at Nancy and said, "I will go over there and see if we can pray for him. If he says OK I will signal you to come over."

On my way to his table, the dread was so thick you could have cut it with a knife. I walked up to the table, stuck out my hand and introduced myself.

The curmudgeon introduced himself as Todd and said, "Well, Jeff, remind me when we met. I have forgotten."

I said, "We just met for the first time." Decision time, what do I do?

I took a deep breath and said, "Todd, the Holy Spirit has had his eye on you for several weeks, at least. God has told me to pray for you on many occasions, which I have not done, and then He would hound me all the way back to Granbury. Would it be alright if my wife and I prayed for you this morning?"

Todd said, "Sure, that would be just fine." The others at his table looked stunned at what was happening.

I motioned for Nancy to join us and introduced her. Then I asked, "You have quite a hitch in your git-along. What's going on there?"

Todd said he had a World War II injury to his back and his knee was "bone-on bone" which combined to make it quite difficult for him to get around.

I explained, "We have seen God do some amazing things with orthopedic problems. Let's see what He will do this morning."

Nancy and I prayed our best prayer. It was quite short primarily because of our discomfort in praying in this surrounding and under these circumstances. When we finished we hit the door running. I told Nancy, "At least God is going to leave me alone on the trip home."

The next time we saw Todd was a few days later. I inquired if there was any improvement in his condition. He reported none. When we saw him move, none was apparent. I told him that we gave "booster shots" if the first prayer didn't work. I hurriedly offered a follow-up prayer and went on my way.

We continued to see Todd a couple times each week. He was never alone again. His attitude and outlook seemed to be sunny and quite different but his pronounced limp and dependence upon his cane continued. He always spoke to us and inquired how we were doing.

For all outward appearances it seemed that nothing had happened when we prayed for Todd. I was glad just to get God off my back in relation to this old man. However, he did seem considerably more social.

After about nine months, Todd approached our table one morning at La Madeleine. He sat with us and said, "You two are such a cute couple. You really go together well."

I said, "Well thanks."

He continued, "I usually go to bed about 8:30 each night, not because I am tired but by then the pain is too much to bear so I get off my feet. While I am in bed, I think about the people in my life who have been important to me. I often think of you two. You will never know how much what you did has meant to me."

With that, he was gone back to his table. Nancy and I looked at each other in tears. Wow. We had thought nothing had happened when we prayed for Todd. Were we ever wrong.

We learned several important lessons in our dealings with Todd. Todd was the first person we prayed for "as we went." He was in our midst but not in our church environment. The impulse to pray for him was significantly different from what we had experienced in the prayer line at church or in healing sessions at our home. No one had brought him to us for prayer. The experience with Todd taught us to be on the lookout for opportunities to pray for God's compassion on His people in everyday situations and unlikely places.

We both believe the circumstances surrounding our relationship with Todd were a test from God to see whether we were really serious about praying for the sick and tormented. After we prayed for Todd, many more everyday opportunities presented themselves. Just like the parable of the minas, God was checking to see what we had done with what He left in our care. When He saw that His mina was earning more minas in our care, He gave us authority in greater situations. (Luke 19:12-26) We apparently had proved trustworthy in a very small matter and greater things were in store for us.

The relationship with Todd reinforced that the sensing of an anointing for healing that is common in the prayer line with the organ playing in the background was unnecessary when God is delivering His compassion to His people. We knew that we have been given authority to pray for people who are sick or suffering irrespective of whether we first sense the presence of God or His healing power.

We know that all believers have been given this authority. How do we know? Because He said so. "Anyone who has faith in me will do those things I have been doing. He will do even greater things than these because I am going to the Father." (John 14:12) "As the Father has sent me, I am sending you." (John 20:21)

We also learned that God is not limited by what we ask for. We asked for relief from physical symptoms. God manifested delivery from torment in Todd's life. That's why Paul described God as "him who is able to do immeasurably more than all we ask or imagine, according to his power that is at work within us." (Ephesians 3:20) Our limitations did not limit God's power.

We also learned that it is impossible for nothing to happen when we pray consistent with God's will. Although we saw no immediate result, and never saw any result that we asked for, there is no question that Todd's life was changed. He was no longer a curmudgeon. We are really glad that the initial disappointment of not seeing the result we hoped for did not prevent us from praying for others as we go.

CHAPTER EIGHTEEN
Persisting In Prayer

J esus told his disciples the parable of the unjust judge "*to show them that they should always pray and not give up.*" (Luke 18:1) After reciting the parable, Jesus said,

> "*And will not God bring about justice for his chosen ones, who cry out to him day and night? Will he keep putting them off? I tell you, he will see that they get justice, and quickly. However, when the Son of Man comes, will he find faith on the earth?*" (Luke 18:7-8)

In the realm of supernatural healing and delivery from torment, *justice* can only be given when Jesus receives what He bought and paid for. Since both healing and delivery from torment are in the atonement, they are *already established* in the kingdom. *Justice* in the kingdom requires that Jesus receive what He has already redeemed.

Jesus ends His explanation of the parable with a question. Will the Son of Man find faith on the earth upon his return? Jesus asked whether upon His return he would find people filled with and acting upon faith. Those who are filled with faith believe that healing and delivery from torment are present day realities in the kingdom, waiting to be manifested in our bodies and souls. The price has been paid. The manifestation awaits. Any delay in the manifestation does not negate what has already been established.

What is a present day reality which has not yet manifested? If we limit our concept of salvation to a change of destination from hell to heaven, that change of destination is a present day reality in the kingdom because Jesus paid the price by His death on the cross and resurrection. However, the manifestation of this present day reality awaits the confession of the believer that Jesus is Lord and the belief that God raised Jesus from the dead. (Romans 10:9) The Apostle Paul described this confession as a "word of faith." (Romans 10:8) It is this faith that causes a change in destination.

Just as a change in destination is not manifested until we confess the "word of faith," physical healing or delivery from torment are not yet manifested, but are equally available. Jesus wanted to know whether upon His return He would find His people exercising their faith in the unseen. *"Now faith is being sure of what we hope for and certain of what we do not see."* (Hebrews 11:1) We are to be as sure of our physical healing and delivery from torment as we are sure of our change in destination.

When a believer utters the "word of faith," Jesus does not then decide whether He will change the believer's destination. It is already in place. In the exact same fashion, when there is a prayer for healing or delivery from torment, Jesus does not then decide whether the Father is both willing and able to heal or deliver from torment. "We do not persist in prayer in order to change God's mind." (Bill Johnson, *Healing, Our Neglected Birthright*)

Matters which are already established in the kingdom do not necessarily manifest themselves in our lives. Jesus came to His own people. They did not receive Him. *"Yet to all who received him, to those who believed in his name, he gave the right to become children of God – children born not of natural descent, nor of human decision or a husband's will, but born of God."* John 1:12-13) The sins of all have been forgiven by Jesus' death and resurrection. That forgiveness is available but must be received. God gave us, through Jesus' death and resurrection, the *right* to become His children. When I exercised that right, Jesus did not come again to die for the forgiveness of my sins. It was already done.

When we pray for divine healing or delivery from torment, it is already done. We are simply asking for a manifestation of the truth already established in the kingdom.

God's response to prayer is not conditioned upon our current behavior. Rather, His response depends entirely upon His great mercy. Daniel prayed for Jerusalem and God's people, saying,

> *"O Lord, in keeping with all your righteous acts, turn away*
> *your anger and your wrath from Jerusalem, your city, your*

holy hill. Our sins and the iniquities of our fathers have made Jerusalem and your people an object of scorn to all those around us. Now, our God, hear the prayers and petitions of your servant. For your sake, O Lord, look with favor on your desolate sanctuary. Give ear, O God, and hear; open your eyes and see the desolation of the city that bears your Name. We do not make requests of you because we are righteous, but because of your great mercy. O Lord, listen! O Lord, forgive! O Lord, hear and act! For your sake, O my God, do not delay, because your city and your people bear your Name. (Daniel 9:16-19)

Daniel was exactly correct. *"We do not make requests of you because we are righteous, but because of your great mercy."*

While Daniel was still speaking and praying, Gabriel appeared and said,

"Daniel, I have now come to give you insight and understanding. As soon as you began to pray, an answer was given, which I have come to tell you, for you are highly esteemed." (Daniel 9:22-23)

God heard Daniel's prayers *as soon as he began to pray.* The response to that prayer was delivered through Gabriel immediately. Healing is sometimes like that. In many instances complete and total healing manifests itself as soon as we begin to pray.

We have often experienced instances when healing manifests itself in those who are praying while they are praying for someone else. At the conclusion of the prayer, the persons praying discover they have likewise received healing or delivery from torment without any request by anyone at the time. It is a collateral blessing.

Other times, healing manifests at a later time. Until the manifestation comes, we are to be persistent in prayer. God is neither bored nor tired of hearing from us.

Daniel experienced a delayed response to his prayer also. Daniel was given a revelation which he did not understand. He sought an explanation from God. The understanding for the revelation was given to him in a vision delivered later. Daniel mourned for three weeks waiting for the explanation. After three weeks, Gabriel appeared to Daniel again. Gabriel explained,

> *"Do not be afraid, Daniel. Since the first day that you set your mind to gain understanding and to humble yourself before your God, your words were heard, and I have come in response to them. But the prince of the Persian kingdom resisted me twenty-one days. Then Michael, one of the chief princes, came to help me, because I was detained there with the king of Persia."* (Daniel 10:12-13)

Just as in the prior encounter with Gabriel, Daniel was assured that God heard his prayers on *"the first day [he] set [his] mind to gain understanding."* Just as in the prior encounter, God sent Gabriel immediately. However, Gabriel encountered resistance in the spirit realm. Michael was then dispatched to assist Gabriel to escape from his encounter with the liar. The result was a delay from the request until the delivery of the requested understanding. The understanding had already been given in the kingdom but had not yet manifested itself to Daniel because of resistance in the spirit realm.

Any understanding of why there may be a delay between the prayer for healing and the manifestation of the already present healing is elusive. The two experiences Daniel had are illustrative of the fact that sometimes the response is quick and complete and other times, the final result awaits further developments. God was not waiting on Daniel to do anything more than ask. The day he asked for understanding, Gabriel was dispatched. The delay was not on God's end and not necessarily on Daniel's end. All we really are told is that there was spiritual resistance by the liar which held up the manifestation for a season.

The parable of the persistent neighbor instructs us to keep on asking. In explaining that parable, Jesus said,

> *"So I say to you: Ask and it will be given to you; seek and you will find; knock and the door will be opened to you. For everyone who asks receives; he who seeks finds; and to him who knocks, the door will be opened."* (Luke 11:9-10; Matthew 7:7-8)

In this context, the wording is ask – and *keep on asking*; seek – and *keep on seeking*; knock – and *keep on knocking*. Do not assume that a delay between your asking and your receiving implies a withholding of God's favor.

Jesus told this parable to his disciples as part of his teaching them how to pray. (Luke 11:1) We are to persist in our prayers.

In 1967 I started experiencing repeated sublaxations of my left shoulder as result of participation in high school football. Sublaxation is a medical term for an incomplete or partial dislocation. In my instance, my left shoulder would "pop" out of place and then return immediately.

These sublaxations in high school were not painful. It was just weird. By 1967 the sublaxations were happening about fifteen times a day but now were accompanied by excruciating pain. Upon my doctor's advice, I underwent a putti-plat procedure to tighten the shoulder joint. For several years I had little problem with my shoulder. I was instructed to avoid any work which would require lifting anything over my head. My range of motion in raising my arm was somewhat limited.

By 1977, all of the old symptoms and pain from the sublaxations had returned. I underwent a Bristow bone block surgery which moved bone and my biceps tendon from the top of my shoulder to a location below the shoulder where the bone was attached with a screw. The result was that my arm was rotated inward and the shoulder was much tighter. Once again, I was instructed not to do work over my head and my range of motion was even more restricted.

I vividly recall the disappointment I felt when all of my friends began lifting their hands in prayer and praise during worship services. I tried but was unable to make my left arm perform satisfactorily to me. When I was watching a performance by Terry Talbot in 1978 I prayed for an increase in my range of motion so that I could raise both hands above my head without restriction. Although I tried, I just didn't have the ability to raise my left arm as high as I thought it should go.

By 1996 I was again experiencing significant problems with my left shoulder. The pain upon sublaxation was debilitating. The frequency of sublaxation and the attendant pain were sufficient for me to ask Nancy to push me in a wheel chair if we had a lot of walking to do. Simply swinging my arm would cause the shoulder to sublax and I would be on the ground from the pain.

On March 19, 1996, I had a total shoulder replacement with placement of an artificial joint. The doctor explained to me that there was significant risk of nerve damage because of the excessive amount of scar tissue he expected from the two prior surgeries.

In part to test for any potential nerve damage, the surgeon informed me that he would be putting my left hand on top of my head following my surgery. The night of the surgery, the doctor was successful in placing my left hand on my head, indicating no mechanical block to that motion. He then told me that the next day he would be by to see me at which time he expected me to do the same. He instructed Nancy how to help me with my "rehab" the next day in getting that left hand to the top of my head.

Nancy and I were faithful in attempting to get my left hand to the top of my head – to no avail. When the surgeon visited late in the day, all I could do was to get my left hand about mouth high. In spite of my best efforts, it simply would not go higher. It was not pain which kept me from lifting my hand. It simply wouldn't go at my command. The surgeon could put my left hand on my head. Nancy could put my left hand on my head. I could only put my left hand on my head if I lifted it with my right hand.

Through the coming months it became apparent that I had experienced significant nerve damage in the area of my left shoulder. The anterior, lateral and posterior portion of my left deltoid muscle "disappeared" within short order. Over time, the adjoining muscles atrophied. I quickly became alarmed with the appearance of my entire left side. The bones in my shoulder were very apparent and the muscles simply were missing. My shoulder was a source of wonder for the massage therapists who worked on me because so much was simply "missing."

In addition to my inability to lift my left arm, I could not reach out to my left side and certainly not behind my body with my left arm. The motion just was not there. Drive up windows for cars found me turning in my seat to pay or receive my food with my right hand. To a very real extent, the world simply ceased to exist on the left side of my body. I would have to turn until the target was in front of me and then I was in business again.

In spite of these limitations, the surgery was a total success. I did not hurt. My shoulder did not sublax. I could walk without discomfort. I could work out with weights. I had no problems with left arm curls with significant weight. I had no problem with left arm triceps exercises. My left arm was as strong as my right in lifting. I just couldn't put my hand high enough to get it on top of my head without using my other hand to assist. Consequently, I could not turn down my collar on my shirt after tying my tie. Little aggravations – nothing major.

Periodically between 1996 and 2009 I would pray for a return of my muscles and the ability to lift my left arm above what little I could muster with the remaining muscles. I would then try to get that arm going to no avail.

Nancy and I attended a conference at Sojourn Church in Carrolton, Texas, in 2008 to listen to Bill Johnson. We wanted to see people healed. We went to study his methods. We went with great anticipation of seeing God act in a way we had not experienced. We did not go with an anticipation that either of us would be healed.

Upon conclusion of his message, Bill gave a word of knowledge that God was going to be healing artificial joints. Nancy had artificial joints in several of her fingers and had undergone nine surgeries for those problems. I had my artificial left shoulder. We hoped we were in for a surprise.

Bill invited those in the congregation to pray for healing. Nancy and I both lifted our hands signifying that we were included in those for whom there had been a word of knowledge. One man prayed for Nancy and two different guys prayed for me.

The man praying for Nancy uttered a simple prayer. "Well, God, heal her hands." He didn't waste time on flowery prayers.

The men praying for me were, apparently, pros. They had very flowery sounding prayers and prayed with great conviction, including commanding my muscles and shoulder to do what they were supposed to do.

Nancy experienced a significant healing in her fingers. She was able to make a fist for the first time in many, many years. She was able to do tasks which require some dexterity which had gradually eluded her through the years. Best for me, she was able to resume complete and total charge of the housework where I lived. That was a miracle.

I, on the other hand, received nothing. My shoulder appeared to be entirely unchanged. I did my best to fight through the disappointment of not being healed in my shoulder by rejoicing in the healing of Nancy's hands. The next night, I did receive a significant healing for my back pain – but that's another story.

By 2010, we had "progressed" in our home group to the point where we were experiencing significant, miraculous healings on a regular basis. Sunday night at our house was a very exciting time for us. We were seeing miracles through the week in restaurants and places of business. We were seeing miracles at our home. We even saw some miracles at church.

In early August, 2010, I asked for prayer to heal my shoulder. I was reluctant to ask for fear that, just as the many times prior, nothing would happen. But, I asked again. I am not certain I believed anything would happen but I was hopeful.

I could discern no immediate change in my shoulder after the prayer. I did my best to lift my arm but did not feel there was any improvement in my ability.

The following week, we prayed again. The man with his hands on my back and shoulder commented that there was more mass in the shoulder area than when he prayed the week before. I thought I was seeing my shoulder muscles fill in but was afraid it was simply hopeful thinking.

After prayer that night, I could do no more than before. I was battling with myself to continue asking for prayer. My desire was to ask – and keep on asking.

On the eighteenth day after the first prayer for my shoulder I was in a swimming pool. Since 1996 the only stoke I could perform was the breast stroke. It was quite abbreviated because I couldn't get my left arm to go very far to my side. I started doing the breast stroke in the pool that day and noticed that I could make a more complete stroke. I stood in the water and moved my arm forward and backward around my body with significantly more range of motion than I had previously. I didn't say anything to Nancy at that time.

That night I was lying on my right side on the couch watching TV. I started talking to Nancy about the experience in the pool that afternoon and soon realized that I was scratching the top of my head with my left hand. I looked at Nancy and said, "I don't think I can do that!"

She assured me that indeed I could not do that.

She encouraged me to stand up and try to put my hand on the top of my head. I found that the muscles were fairly spastic and my arm seemed quite heavy but I could get my hand to the top of my head.

Through the next several weeks, I stretched aggressively to stretch out the muscles which had contracted significantly, limiting my range of motion. As those muscles relaxed and stretched, I had more and more range of motion. The more I put my hand on top of my head, the better coordinated I was and the less effort it took.

The progress in my left shoulder continues. The muscle continues to fill in. The healing is manifesting itself to sight. The strength continues to get better. The healing is manifesting itself in more controlled and smooth motion.

I was asked to give my testimony concerning the healing of my shoulder in church. Upon hearing that testimony, one of the members of the congregation experienced a healing of a similar problem in her shoulder. She went home and watched the pod-cast of the service with her husband who had not accompanied her to church that day. While watching again, she experienced even more healing. The testimony of Jesus is the spirit of prophecy.

In November, we again went to Sojourn Church in Carrolton to see Bill Johnson. During the worship on Friday night, I felt intense pain in the area where my lateral deltoid muscle had been. When I looked at my arm I noticed that my arm completely filled the sleeve of my shirt. I turned to Nancy and said, "My arm is killing me. I think it is growing."

On Saturday of that week, Bill Johnson announced that God was healing long standing conditions caused by trauma. I felt that I was included in that description. I received prayer in three short bursts that night. At the end of the prayer that night, I could lift my left arm over my head in a motion similar to a "jumping jack." This was way cool.

I cannot explain how, why or when my shoulder was healed. I can report Who did it – and it wasn't me or my friends who prayed for me. I am confident that God heard the prayers from the beginning. I am confident that He never gave up on me or my condition. I am confident that my healing continues to manifest to this day and will do so in the future.

I don't know whether battles were being waged in the spirit realm over the healing God sent my way. I can only report that from 1996 to 2010 I was unable to put my left hand on the top of my head without using my other hand to lift it – and now I can.

Do not be discouraged if there is not an immediate manifestation of healing or delivery from torment. Ask – and keep on asking. Seek – and keep on seeking. Knock – and keep on knocking.

I have been impressed for the last two years to tell people who have conditions that have lasted for a long time that God is not done with them. I believe the passage of time is not an indicator that God has given up on the condition. I do not believe the passage of time indicates that God is trying to teach us a lesson before healing us.

What I can tell you for sure is that I didn't learn any lesson that opened the door to God healing my shoulder. The healing that has come and continues to improve was purchased on Jesus' way to the cross. It is now manifesting itself in my body.

There are many who have had long standing conditions for which we have prayed. Out experience is that:

- those people whose legs have grown out to be even with the other leg while we watched have a had a short leg for quite a while – but no more;

- the man who had pain in his knee had that pain for more than fifteen years – and now it is gone;
- the man who had a metal rod and eight screws in his ankle which prevented the ankle from flexing had been in that condition eight years – and now he can move the ankle with no restrictions;
- the people who have had tingling and burning pain in their lower legs and feet have been in that condition for many years – and the tingling and burning is gone;
- the lady with scoliosis in her back that caused one leg to manifest as shorter than the other and caused her back pain had been that way for many years – and now she is pain free with two legs the same length.
- the woman with profound deafness who can now hear had been deaf for quite a while – now she can hear; and
- those people who have been freed from torment were tormented for quite a while – but now they are free.

It is a continual fight not to let disappointment lead to abandonment of hope. I am convinced that God is never satisfied when one of His children is oppressed by the devil. He has never stopped acting on behalf of His children. Expect a miracle at any moment, even when many moments have already passed. He's not done!

CHAPTER NINETEEN

The Testimony of Jesus

D o you want to know God's will on any matter? Simply look at Jesus – He is it.

"In the past God spoke to our forefathers through the prophets at many times and in various ways, but in these last days he has spoken to us by his Son, whom he appointed heir of all things, and through whom he made the universe. The Son is the radiance of God's glory and the exact representation of his being, sustaining all things by his powerful word. After he had provided purification for sins, he sat down at the right hand of the Majesty in heaven." (Hebrews 1:1-3)

God has "spoken to us by his Son." This idea is not limited to the words in red in the Bible. It encompasses all the truth about Jesus' life. The Father *spoke* to us by sending Jesus in a man's body. Jesus, as the Word, speaks through His every action.

Jesus is the *"exact representation"* of the Father. If we want to know the Father's will on any issue, we can simply look at what Jesus did or said in such a circumstance. The Old Testament prophets presented the Word of God as they heard it. Jesus "re-presents" the Father with greater clarity and specific information.

"Jesus Christ is the same yesterday and today and forever." (Hebrews 13:8) If Jesus does not change, we know that the Father does not change. The Father's attitudes and attributes expressed and "re-presented" by Jesus are the same today as when Jesus walked the earth. Importantly, those attitudes and attributes will be the same tomorrow and forever. If the Father did it while Jesus was here, He is still doing it. If the Father said it while Jesus was here, He is still saying it. The testimony of Jesus is the spirit of prophecy. (Revelation 19:10) Nancy and I often recite some of the biblical testimony of Jesus prior to beginning to pray for a condition in order to change the atmosphere to make it more conducive to healing. The spirit of prophecy has power.

The Father's attitudes and attributes have already been spoken by Jesus and are illustrated in His actions. The world would not have room for the books that would need to be written to contain the full account. (John 21:25) So, why are some accounts included and others omitted. It seems likely that the accounts contained in scripture are there to teach us a particular truth. The truths which we have found important in the area of healing include the testimony of Jesus set out below.

God is Willing

A man with leprosy came to Jesus and knelt before him, demonstrating his submission, worship and faith. He knew that Jesus was *able* to cleanse him of his leprosy. "Lord, if you are willing, you can make me clean." The leper did not question Jesus' *ability* to cleanse him. He was convinced that Jesus had both the power and the authority to cleanse him. The leper was questioning whether Jesus was willing to touch an unclean person. He wanted to know whether he was disqualified from God's mercy, grace and favor because the religious establishment considered him unclean.

In the Old Testament, if someone touched a person with leprosy, that person likewise became unclean. When a leper was healed of his leprosy, there were still purification rites and periods of time required to remove the impact of his prior unclean state.

In the New Testament, there is a new sheriff in town. When Jesus touched the leper, the leper was cleansed rather than Jesus becoming unclean. Jesus response was sure and swift. He touched the leper and declared "I am willing. Be clean." The leper was cured and cleansed immediately. (Matthew 8:1-4; Luke 5:12-13; and Mark 2:40-42) The Jerusalem Bible translates Jesus' response as *"Of course I am willing."* What an assurance! Of course Jesus is willing to heal. Of course Jesus is willing to enter our unclean condition and restore us to a clean condition.

By this account we can be certain that God is willing to cleanse all, even those considered unclean by the religious community. All that is required is the touch of God. The leper did not have to clean up his act. He did not have to repent. He did not have to confess his sins. He simply had to approach Jesus in an attitude of humility and worship with total confidence in His ability. Since Jesus was willing then, we know that He is willing now. He has not changed His mind.

Healing Comes When God Speaks His Word

The Word of God is powerful and all sufficient. There is nothing God cannot do simply by his speaking the desired result into existence. God spoke all creation into existence

Divine healing is made manifest when God says so. After Jesus cleansed the leper, a Roman centurion approached Jesus. (Matthew 8:5-13) The centurion, as a Roman soldier, was not one of God's chosen people but he loved the nation of Israel and had built the local synagogue. (Luke 7:1-10) He told Jesus that one of his servants lay at home paralyzed and in terrible suffering. Jesus immediately set out to go to the servant to heal him.

Jesus did not tell the centurion he needed to convert to the Jewish religion and then come back. He did not inquire about the status of the centurion's heart. He did not tell the centurion to repent. Jesus knew that the centurion had faith in Him and had approached Him in an attitude of humility, displaying total confidence in His ability. Apparently, that was enough.

The centurion was impressed with his own sinful nature. He believed he was not worthy of a visitation from God. Is it possible that his confession of his unworthiness rendered him worthy? He said, *"Lord, I do not deserve to have you come under my roof. But just say the word, and my servant will be healed."*

Jesus said, *"'Go! It will be done just as you believed it would.' And his servant was healed at that very hour."* (Matthew 8:13)

Jesus saw that the Father was healing the centurion's servant of both his paralysis and his terrible suffering. Jesus did not lay hands on him. He did not inquire about the state of the servant's spirit. He did not require any action from the servant. He did not inquire whether the servant would repent if he were healed. He simply declared the will of the Father.

The requested healing and delivery from suffering was done *at the time it was announced.* The servant was healed *"at that very hour."* Nothing more than the declaration was required.

Jesus Took Up Our Infirmities and Carried Our Diseases

Jesus went from the encounter with the centurion to Peter's house where He found Peter's mother in law lying in bed with a fever. With no apparent request and no preamble, Jesus touched her hand and the fever left her. What are we supposed to do when we receive a touch from Jesus? Exactly what Peter's mother-in-law did! "She got up and began to wait on him." (Matthew 8:14-17; Mark 2:29-34 and Luke 4:38-41)

That evening *many* who were demon possessed and those who were sick were brought to Jesus. Jesus drove out the spirits with a word and healed *all* the sick. Jesus had authority and power to destroy the works of the devil (1 John 3:8), irrespective of whether the problem was an afflicting spirit or simply a disease from the devil.

The testimony of Jesus' healing the leper, the centurion's servant and Peter's mother in law created an atmosphere in which those healings would be duplicated. Jesus was testifying by His actions that God is in the healing business – and business is good.

Matthew's gospel explains that *"this was to fulfill what was spoken through the prophet Isaiah: 'He took up our infirmities and carried our diseases.'"* (Matthew 8:17) In those days Jesus was taking up our infirmities and carrying our diseases. On His way to the cross, Jesus made a payment for our healing and delivery from torment. In the kingdom, Jesus has already completely dealt with our infirmities and diseases. His action is still sufficient.

We Are to be Specific

As Jesus was leaving Jericho two blind men were in the large crowd following him. One of them was blind Bartimaeus. (Matthew 20, 29-35; Mark 10:46-52; Luke 18:35-43) As they sat by the roadside and heard that Jesus was going by, they shouted, "Lord, Son of David, have mercy on us!" Even though the crowd sought to quiet them, they shouted all the louder.

When Jesus heard the request (or was it a demand?), He asked Bartimaeus *"What do you want me to do for you?"*

Talk about a blank check. These blind men could have asked for any and every blessing that God was capable of delivering. They asked for too little. *"'Lord,' they answered, 'we want our sight.'"*

What if they had asked for more? What if they had asked for revelation knowledge? What if they had asked for wisdom as Solomon did? Would God have granted them their sight in addition? We will never know. Instead, they asked only for their sight.

"Jesus had compassion on them." (Matthew 20:34) When Jesus delivers God's compassion by bringing peace, comfort and blessing to God's people, it is good news in the kingdom. However, there is a corresponding direct attack on the enemy. Every healing, every delivery from torment is another opportunity for God to demonstrate, once again, Jesus' victory over the devil.

In the account of this incident in Mark's Gospel, Jesus said, "your faith has healed you." Not only did Bartimaeus have faith, he put some legs to his faith. He fought the large crowd and sat by the roadside waiting for Jesus. He sought Jesus at the top of his voice and repeatedly. In spite of being rebuked by the crowd, he repeated his request until Jesus responded. Did Jesus hear him the first time but test his resolve by waiting for the demonstrated persistence? We simply do not know. What we do know is that he had "enough faith" to be persistent, in the very face of condemnation by the crowd.

Luke records that Bartimaeus *"followed Jesus, praising God. When all the people saw it, they also praised God."* Why did the crowd praise God for this healing? In other instances, the response of the crowd was ambivalent, some believing and others questioning. Did Bartimaeus' praise create an atmosphere in which the power of God was made more manifest? Was it his praise that led *"all the people [who] saw it"* to also praise God? There may be something very powerful in a healing coupled with praise.

Faith Coupled With Action Matters

When Jesus was on his way to raise Jairus' daughter from the dead, a woman with her own problems approached Him from behind. (Matthew 9:18-26; Mark 5:22-43) She may not have known that Jesus was on a mission. Perhaps she knew of the mission and did not want to interrupt. In any event, she "blind-sided" Jesus to secure a blessing for herself. She had confidence if she could only touch his cloak, the power residing in Him could heal her of the issue of blood which had persisted for twelve years. Surely, she was desperate by this time. She had been under the care of many doctors and had spent all she had. In spite of it all, she continued to grow worse. (Mark 5:26)

When she touched his cloak, Jesus turned and saw her. He realized that "*power had gone out from him*" and turned, searching for the problem. (Mark 5:30) He knew that the Father was dealing with a circumstance requiring His compassion, knew that He was to participate and took the time to find the object of God's compassion. After asking His disciples who had touched His clothes, Jesus "*kept looking around to see who had done it.*" (Mark 5:32) The woman knew that "*she was freed from her suffering*" even before Jesus realized that power had gone out from him. (Mark 5:29)

Jesus spoke with the woman. She explained the "whole truth" to the one who is The Truth. He said to her, "*Daughter, your faith has healed you. Go in peace and be freed from your suffering.*" (Mark 5:34) When we pursue Jesus, He will pursue us to announce our freedom from our suffering. Jesus is never too busy working on other problems to be bothered by us. He is never too busy that He will not respond to our faith, especially when it is coupled with action.

Meanwhile, Jairus had been waiting, probably not so patiently. After all, his daughter was dying and Jesus wanted to know who had touched him! While Jesus was still talking to the woman, someone from Jairus' house came to him and reported, "*Your daughter is dead. Don't bother the teacher any more.*" (Luke 8:49) When Jesus heard this, He comforted Jairus, "Don't be afraid; just believe and she will be healed." (Luke 8:50) This message to Jairus was the ultimate "two-fer." Jesus told the woman, in Jairus' presence, that her faith had healed her and then assured Jairus that if he would just believe, his daughter would likewise be healed.

Jairus now had a dilemma. He has been told that his daughter has died. In spite of that report, Jesus is telling him that if he will just believe his daughter will be healed. Who was Jairus to believe – the people from his own household or Jesus the stranger? Jairus made the right choice. He believed Jesus was good for His word and his daughter was healed.

Jesus Wants to Know Your Desires

Jesus healed an invalid beside the pool at Bethesda. (John 5:1-15) The pool-side was a gathering spot for disabled people. Irrespective of whatever had happened at Bethesda before Jesus came by, all of those people who came there regularly were having their needs met in a non-supernatural manner. Some form of good works was in operation at that place. Perhaps this was the meeting place for the first Kiwanis Club.

Few, if any, were being cured each day there. The angel only *"went down at a certain season into the pool and troubled the water."* (John 5:4 KJV) The angel, apparently, was not there every day – or even in every season. When the angel did trouble the water, only the first "whosoever" was made whole of "whatsoever disease he had." If you weren't first, you were left out.

Jesus approached a man who had been an invalid for thirty-eight years. We don't know how many of those years he had lain by the pool. We do know he was there that day, armed with his excuses why he would not be healed. In spite of having his excuses ready why he would not be healed that day, he returned (or remained). In a very real sense, he was simply working the program. Somehow his needs would be met for another day if he could just get to the pool.

"Jesus saw him lying there and learned that he had been in this condition for a long time." (John 5:6) The "condition" he had been in for a long time included a certain knowledge that he had *"no one to help [him] into the pool when the water is stirred"* and that *"someone else goes down ahead of"* him. (John 5:7)

Jesus was dealing with a member of the institutional sick. This man's job was to be an invalid, which did not include getting healed. He likely had no job skills. He likely had no ambitions. Did he want to start earning a living? Did he want to develop job skills? Was he willing to work for the rest of his life?

Jesus asked the relevant question. *"Do you want to get well?"* (John 5:6) The answer for this man, and for many who are "thriving" in their current condition, is not easy. Getting well had many implications in addition to the end (or maybe only amelioration) of the specific condition causing him to be an invalid. Did the offer of getting well carry with it job training? Did the offer carry with it any assurance that today's and tomorrow's needs would be met by the good deeds of the civic minded? Could getting cured of his invalid condition be a death sentence?

We don't know if this man had ever walked. If he had ever walked, he had not walked in thirty-eight years. Yet, Jesus told him to *"Get up! Pick up your mat and walk."* Since it was the Sabbath, Jewish law prohibited him from picking up his mat. The law also had very stringent limits on how far he could walk on that day and for what purpose. Yet, Jesus commanded him to get back in the game – no matter the impact on organized religion. What did it take to obey in the face of the apparent requirements of the law?

There is a measure of faith involved in this healing. Jesus' command to get up required a bushel of faith for the man to even try to get up. Perhaps he was being commanded to do something he had never learned to do. Surely, he was being commanded to do something he had not anticipated on that day (or any other). Yet, he rose! He could have lay by the pool and looked at Jesus with a tilt of his head like the RCA dog. He could have asked himself if this guy was for real. Instead, he was fully persuaded that Jesus was able to equip him to do what Jesus commanded him to do. Whatever measure of faith he exhibited was sufficient.

There is sometimes reluctance in the institutional sick to seek healing. Perhaps the curse of medical diagnosis has been fully received and interferes with faith. Perhaps the fear of not being healed and any resultant judgment on the individual's worthiness (or not) is too great. No matter the source of the impediment, Jesus wanted to know whether the invalid wanted to be well. There is a difference in wanting to get well and wanting to be healed miraculously. A person may well *not believe* in miraculous healing and still be healed.

It seems less likely that a person who does not *want to get well* would receive a miraculous healing. If the person does not want to get well, there is an emotional component which must be addressed in addition to the physical need. First comes the delivery from torment of not wanting to get well. Then comes the manifestation of the physical healing.

Check It Out

Some people brought a blind man to Jesus at Bethsaida and begged Jesus to touch him. (Mark 8: 22-25) Jesus spit on the man's eyes outside the village and put his hands on him. Jesus then asked him, *"Do you see anything?"* (Mark 8:23) Why did Jesus check to determine the result? Because of Jesus' self-imposed limitations, He did not know whether the man could see. He did know that the Father was healing the blind. Isaiah's prophecy said so. (Luke 4:18-19)

The blind man reported seeing men as trees, walking. *"Once more Jesus put his hands on the man's eyes."* (Mark 8:25) When the man opened his eyes after this second touch, his sight had been restored.

Jesus checked to see if the healing was complete. Jesus was not demonstrating a lack of faith when He made His inquiry. Likewise, it is not a lack of faith for us to ask whether God's compassion has been delivered to its target. Jesus' prayer and action needed repetition. Are we too proud to repeat our request? Good enough for Jesus should be good enough for me.

These principles should shape our prayer life as well as our expectations. We should be encouraged to know that not only did Jesus bear our infirmities and carry our diseases, He is willing and able to act today and forever just as He did in biblical times. We should remember that Jesus wants to know whether we want to get well. If we want to get well, what, specifically, do we want Him to do? No matter the report, Jesus says, "Don't be afraid, just believe."

APPENDIX:
The Cessation Argument

Do you believe that God is still in the supernatural healing business. Perhaps you have been taught that the Holy Spirit is no longer performing in that fashion. Your participation in divine healing depends in large part on resolution of a debate which has been "on-going" between theologians and bible scholars for many years.

There is no debate for me. God is in the supernatural healing business today – and business is good! Some believe that God provides healing exclusively through the hands of doctors and medicines. I know better.

Most Christians have not been exposed directly to cessationist theories. In the absence of man's teaching, the everyday believer may find himself anywhere along a continuum from one extreme to another:

- God no longer heals supernaturally;
- God acts through doctors and medicine only;
- God heals through special envoys who have "the touch"; and
- Sickness and disease is a product of man's mind.

Some advocate that God the Father used miraculous healings, signs and wonders to give His stamp of approval to Jesus. According to this position, miracles validated Jesus as the Son of God. Once Jesus was validated, there was no longer a need for signs, wonders and miraculous healing. This theology posits that God is no longer in the supernatural healing business because Jesus has been validated.

"Cessationists" teach that divine healing and miracles are not for today. In 1934 there was a famous debate between Elder Ben M. Bogard, pastor of the Antioch Missionary Baptist Church, Little Rock, Arkansas, and Aimee Semple McPherson, founder of the Four Square Gospel Church, which had its headquarters at Angelus Temple, Los Angeles, California. Dr. Bogard was a cessationist. Mrs. McPherson was on the other side. The debate was stenographically reported by J. E. Rhodes and is available on many internet sites today. (See for example, *www.padfield.com*)

The proposition for the debate was:

> "Divine healing and miracles as taught and manifest in the Word of God ceased with the Apostolic Age."

Dr. Bogard argued that "Holy Rollerism, Pentecostalism, McPhersonism," modern miracles, divine healing, speaking with tongues and other manifestations of the Holy Spirit were "heresies." Dr. Bogard was not impressed with Aimee McPherson's ministry and was certain there was great danger in her teaching.

Cessationists argue that God used miracles, signs and wonders to validate a messenger. If signs and wonders followed a preacher, he could be trusted. They argue that the canonization of the New Testament now furnishes the means for validation of a messenger. The availability of the written word of God rendered it unnecessary for God to confirm the spoken word to bring faith to unbelievers through miraculous demonstrations of God's power. Dr. Bogard argued that once the Bible was fully confirmed, preachers of the Word of God could be gauged by study of the New Testament. Demonstrations of the power of God were no longer needed to confirm the Word as preached. Dr. Bogard argued that miracles were done away with when they were no longer needed, just like the Jewish ceremonies performed in the Temple and the animal sacrifices of the Old Testament.

Dr. Bogard relied on Paul's first letter to the Corinthians to support his claim that healing, prophecy, the word of knowledge and tongues, were "done away" when the New Testament was completed. (1 Corinthians 13:10) "But when the New Testament was completed they had the perfect thing, the perfect law of liberty, and then inspiration, prophecy, tongues and all other miracles were done away." (Dr. Bogard's first speech in the Bogard - McPherson Debate) My personal experience repeatedly testifies that he was wrong.

In essence, Dr. Bogard argued that Jesus was no longer in the healing business because that business had become irrelevant and unnecessary. This argument flies in the face of Hebrews 13:8: *"Jesus Christ is the same yesterday and today and forever.*" Jesus performed miracles as part of God's plan to deliver His compassion to His people. (Mark 1:41) God is still delivering compassion to His people. If Jesus healed all who came to Him as an expression of the Father's compassion, He continues to heal those who come to Him today out of that same compassion. Otherwise Jesus could not be the same "today and forever" as He was "yesterday."

Signs Accompany

The plan of salvation is simple. "Whoever" believes the good news will be saved while those who do not believe will be condemned. Actually, those who do not believe are condemned already. (Mark 16:15-16; John 3:17-18)

Jesus promised that signs would accompany those who believe. Jesus promised that believers would cast out devils in his name and lay hands on the sick and the sick would recover. (Mark 16:17-18) Unless Jesus' promise is good to this day, He cannot be "the same yesterday and today and forever."

Signs Are Not Limited to the Apostles

Dr. Bogard argued that the words "these signs" referred exclusively to the signs the Apostles did. That is, the signs God performed through the Apostles, as recorded in the Bible, were to be considered the *exclusive* signs that shall accompany those who believe. Once the Apostles were gone, there were to be no more signs.

The enormity of the error of this entire argument can scarcely be comprehended. First, Jesus said, "These signs will accompany those who believe." (Mark 16:17) He did not say these signs will accompany the Apostles. He said the signs would accompany those who believe. People did not stop coming to saving faith in Jesus at the death of the last Apostle. Even today, people are being saved by believing in Jesus. Jesus' promise has not been revoked. Signs will accompany those who believe.

Second, Jesus was made manifest to destroy the works of the devil. (1 John 3:8) God anointed Jesus with the Holy Spirit and with power so that He could heal all who were oppressed by the devil. (Acts 10:38) Jesus promised that *"anyone who has faith in me will do what I have been doing. He will do even greater things than these, because I am going to the Father."* (John 14:12)

Since Jesus was in the business of healing all who were oppressed by the devil when He walked this earth, He is still in that business – or else He is not the same. If *anyone* who has faith in Jesus *will do* what He had been doing, He must still be in the business of miracles, signs and wonders – or else He is a liar. The promise is not addressed to the Apostles but rather to *anyone who has faith* in Him.

God, in His compassion, sent Jesus to free His children from the devastating effects of the works of the devil – sickness, disease and torment. Who are these children of God who are to receive God's compassion? "Yet to all who received him, to those who believed in his name, he gave the right to become children of God." (John 1:12) For those who believe in His name, Jesus' actions and sacrifice gave us the right to *become* children of God. God is our benevolent Father, bestowing on us His good gifts. (Matthew 7:7-11) Forgiveness of our sins, healing of our infirmities and delivery from torment all spring from the compassion of God.

Dr. Bogard's Devil Was Too Big

Dr. Bogard refused to believe *anyone* had been healed through the ministry of Aimee McPherson. If anyone had been, he was certain that God did not do the healing. Indeed, he stated, "since God withdrew the power to work miracles from his people it follows that any miracles wrought now are wrought by the power of the devil and not by the power of God." (Dr. Bogard's First Speech, Bogard – McPherson Debate) That is, if any were healed, the devil did it, not God.

This argument may come as a great shock to some. Most people believe that it is God who is in the healing business. However, most people do not truly expect that the store is open to all and that the hours of operation are all day, every day. There is an unstated attitude that God is in the healing business, just not for me and mine and not as a result of my asking. Healing is for other people in extraordinary circumstances and can only be accessed through experts God has anointed with special powers. These people believe in a God who is way too small.

The devil simply is not in the business of delivering God's compassion to His people. The works of the devil are sin, sickness, disease and torment. Jesus destroyed the works of the devil and announced from the cross IT IS FINISHED. (John 19:30) Jesus was one hundred percent successful in His mission to destroy the works of the devil. He did not leave matters incomplete.